HOW **TWO** LOVE
IN A BROKEN WORLD

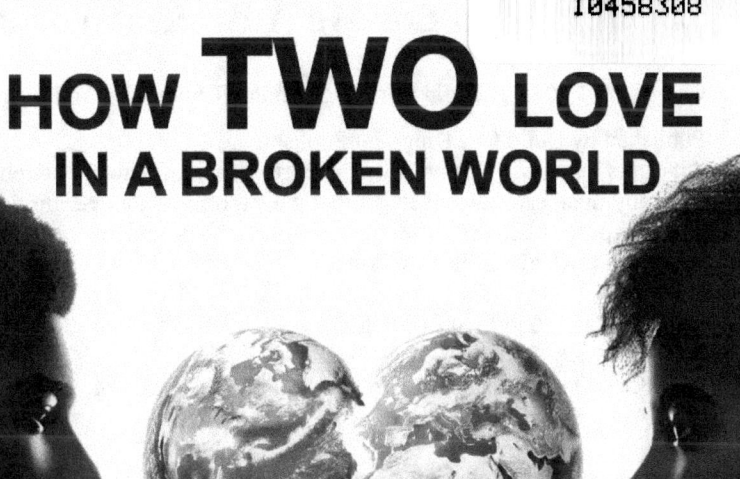

A RELATIONSHIP GUIDE
TO CREATING LOVE IN YOUR WORLD

ALLEN BROWN

RELATIONSHIP COACH FOR OVER 20 YEARS

BUILD OUR KINGDOM PUBLISHING
—— BUILD OUR KINGDOM.COM ——

How Two Love In A Broken World

1st Edition January 2025 First Printing
ISBN for paperback: 978-1-964203-13-3
Build Our Kingdom Publishing, LLC. 560 Main St, Stroudsburg, PA 18360
Edited by: Allen Brown

Scripture taken from the New King James Version®. Copyright © 1982 by Thomas Nelson. Used with permission. All rights reserved.

Scripture quotations marked (NIV) are taken from the Holy Bible, New International Version®, NIV®. Copyright © 1973, 19 78, 1984, 2011 by Biblica, Inc.™ Used by permission of Zondervan. All rights reserved worldwide. www.zondervan.com The "NIV" and "New International Version" are trademarks registered in the United States Patent and Trademark Office by Biblica, Inc™

Although the publisher and the author have made every effort to ensure that the information in this book was correct at press time and while this publication is designed to provide accurate information in regard to the subject matter covered, the publisher and the author assume no responsibility for errors, inaccuracies, omissions, or any other inconsistencies herein and hereby disclaim any liability to any party for any loss, damage, or disruption caused by errors or omissions, whether such errors or omissions result from negligence, accident, or any other cause.

This publication is meant as a source of valuable information for the reader, however, it is not meant as a substitute for direct expert assistance. If such a level of assistance is required, the services of a competent professional should be sought.

Table of Contents

Table of Contents iii

Dedication v

Acknowledgment.. vii

Introduction Understanding Your Broken World........................ 1

Chapter 1 Welcome to the World.. 7

    Exercises for Chapter 1: Welcome to the World.................... 13

Chapter 2 It's a Cold World 17

    Exercises for Chapter 2: It's a Cold World 23

Chapter 3 The World Is Yours 27

    Exercises for Chapter 3: The World Is Yours 33

Chapter 4 Exploring New Worlds 37

    Exercises for Chapter 4: Exploring New Worlds 43

Chapter 5 Creating a New World 47

    Exercises for Chapter 5: Creating a New World 53

Chapter 6 When Worlds Collide 57

    Exercises for Chapter 6: When Worlds Collide 65

Chapter 7 Changing Your World One Goal at a Time 69

    Exercises for Chapter 7: Changing Your World One Goal at a Time 73

Chapter 8 A Vision for Your World 77

    Exercises for Chapter 8: A Vision for Your World................ 83

Chapter 9 Conquering the World Together 87

Exercises for Chapter 9: Conquering the World Together 93

Chapter 10 A New World Order 97

Exercises for Chapter 10: A New World Order 103

Chapter 11 A World of Trouble 107

Exercises for Chapter 11: A World of Trouble 113

Chapter 12 A World of Temptation 117

Exercises for Chapter 12: A World of Temptation 123

Chapter 13 You Rock My World 127

Exercises for Chapter 13: You Rock My World 133

Chapter 14 What in the World Happened? 137

Exercises for Chapter 14: What in the World Happened? 143

Chapter 15 As the World Turns 147

Exercises for Chapter 15: *As the World Turns* 153

Chapter 16 The End of the World 157

Exercises for Chapter 16: The End of the World 163

Final Thoughts Finding Lasting Love in a Broken World 167

About the Author 171

About Build Our Kingdom Publishing 173

Dedication

To Melissa,

I dedicate this book to you, my wife, and to our marriage. Over the past twenty seven years, we have shared a journey that continues to grow stronger despite both of us coming from broken places—some more obvious than others.

Through it all, we've managed to keep moving forward with good goals and a great vision. I believe that God placed you in my life to help me grow as an individual and to become the person I am meant to be, fulfilling my calling and purpose.

You have been a vital part of my life, and I love you.

~ Allen ~

Acknowledgment

First, I want to acknowledge God, who has given me the wisdom to navigate the difficult times in my relationship. I thank You for the insights and understanding You've led me to learn and embrace. I'm grateful for the blessings of marriage, my wife, Melissa, and everything that has come from this union.

To my kids: thank you for the joy and purpose you bring to my life. You remind me why I continue to thrive and pursue my calling. I love each one of you deeply, and I pray God continues to bless you.

To my parents, Carolyn and Elijah Brown: thank you for modeling a relationship of love and commitment for over 41 years. Your example has left a profound impression on my life, and I thank God for the blessing of witnessing your journey.

I thank the many men and women who sought my advice on relationships. Your stories and challenges offered me new insights that also strengthened my own relationship. I thank God for sending you my way and pray I was able to provide guidance and hope.

Finally, to the readers of this book: thank you for taking the time to engage with my story and trust in me to offer guidance for your relationship. I pray that this book inspires you, encourages you, and helps you build the love you deserve in this broken world.

Thank you all, and God bless.

Introduction

Understanding Your Broken World

"How Two Love in a Broken World: A Couple's Guide to Strengthen Love and Repair the Broken Pieces" is a book born out of reflection, experience, and the desire to help couples navigate the complexities of relationships. This book is not only a guide but also a call to awareness—a way to understand the unseen systems that shape us, mold us, and, at times, break us.

Have you ever considered how you exist in someone else's world? Have you pondered what you represent in their world and why they respond to you the way they do? The goal of this book is to open your eyes to this reality: we are all products of our own worlds. And by "world," I do not mean the Earth itself but rather the systems, patterns, and ideologies that constitute the framework of our existence.

From a biblical perspective, the term "world" often refers not to the physical realm but to a collection of systems. The Bible, particularly in passages like Romans 12:2, calls for transformation through the renewing of the mind:

1

"Do not conform to the pattern of this world but be transformed by the renewing of your mind. Then you will be able to test and approve what God's will is—his good, pleasing and perfect will."

Here, the word "world" is derived from the Greek term *cosmos(kosmos)*, which refers to an organized system—patterns that govern how the world operates. It is in this context that the Bible instructs believers not to conform to these worldly patterns but to adopt a new mindset rooted in Christ. Another reference, 1 John 2:15-17, warns believers not to love the world or the things in it because these are not of the Father but are of the world.

When Paul speaks of transformation in Romans, he is urging us to break away from the systems of dysfunction that have shaped our understanding. From birth, we are introduced to systems—family structures, societal norms, educational paradigms, and even cultural biases—that mold our view of the world. These systems become our "normal." For instance, someone raised in a household with a loving, two-parent dynamic will have a vastly different worldview than someone who grew up in a broken or abusive environment. What is familiar to one may feel foreign, even strange, to another.

The Collision of Two Worlds

As individuals, our worldviews are shaped by everything we've seen, experienced, and internalized. From the way our parents raised us (or didn't) to the societal expectations we grew up with, these elements form the subconscious patterns that dictate how we live and interact. Now, imagine what happens when two people from entirely different worlds attempt to build a life together.

Often, these worlds collide. This collision is not just a metaphor but a reality for many couples. Consider a relationship where one partner grew up in a family that emphasized open communication and emotional vulnerability, while the other partner was raised in an environment where emotions were suppressed, and communication was minimal. The clash of these worlds can lead to misunderstandings, frustration, and sometimes even the breakdown of the relationship.

This is why understanding each other's world is crucial. Relationships demand compromise, empathy, and, most importantly, awareness of the "baggage" we bring from our respective worlds. The Bible reminds us in **Amos 3:3**, *"Can two walk together, except they be agreed?"* Agreement—or at least the willingness to seek understanding—is the foundation of any successful relationship.

The Patterns of the World

The Bible often speaks of the "patterns of the world" as something to avoid. These patterns include not only behaviors but also mindsets and systems that are contrary to God's design. For example, in **2 Corinthians 5:17**, Paul writes, *"Therefore, if anyone is in Christ, the new creation has come: The old has gone, the new is here!"* This transformation is not just about spiritual renewal but also about breaking free from the dysfunctions that the world has ingrained in us.

For instance, someone who grew up in a home filled with conflict may subconsciously replicate those patterns in their own relationships. They may not even realize that their behaviors are rooted in a dysfunctional worldview until they are confronted with a different perspective. This is why self-awareness is so critical. Without it, we risk perpetuating the very cycles we seek to escape.

Brokenness: A Universal Truth

As the author, I've come to understand that we are all broken in some way. Some of us carry deeper wounds than others, but none of us are without flaws. This brokenness, however, does not mean we are incapable of building meaningful relationships or leading fulfilling lives. What it does mean is that we need to be intentional about recognizing and addressing the areas where our brokenness may be hindering us.

The enemy, whom the Bible calls "the god of this world" (**2 Corinthians 4:4**), thrives on our brokenness. His goal is to destroy what God has designed to be good—our relationships, our peace, our very identity. **1 Peter 5:8** describes him as a roaring lion, seeking whom he may devour. His strategies are deliberate, and his influence pervasive. From birth, he works to distort our understanding of ourselves and others, creating division where God intends unity.

Sensitivity and Healing

Understanding someone else's broken world requires sensitivity, empathy, and a willingness to step outside of your own worldview. It means recognizing that the person you love may be carrying wounds you cannot see—wounds that influence how they respond to you, how they perceive love, and how they navigate conflict.

For example, someone who grew up in an environment where love was conditional may struggle to believe in unconditional love. Their worldview has taught them to expect rejection or abandonment, even when none is present. As their partner, your role is not to "fix" them but to provide a safe space for healing. This requires patience, prayer, and a deep reliance on God's wisdom.

Moving Forward Together

This book is not just about understanding your partner's world; it is also about understanding your own. It is about identifying the patterns you've adopted, questioning whether they align with God's truth, and being willing to change. The Bible calls this process transformation—a renewal of the mind that allows us to see ourselves and others through God's eyes.

As you read this book, you will discover practical tools for navigating the complexities of relationships. You will learn how to communicate effectively, resolve conflicts, and create a partnership rooted in mutual respect and understanding. More importantly, you will gain a deeper understanding of how God's design for love and relationships can bring healing to even the most broken of worlds.

Chapter 1

Welcome to the World

The story of your life began the moment you were welcomed into this world. Think about it—you didn't choose to be here. You didn't get to select your parents, decide the circumstances of your birth, or shape the environment that would mold your earliest years. You came into this world as part of a design far beyond your control, entrusted to people who were tasked with raising you, even though they themselves were still navigating their own flaws and struggles.

From the very beginning, you were dependent on others—adults who were meant to nurture you, protect you, and provide for your needs. Whether they succeeded or failed, these early caregivers left their mark on you, creating the foundation upon which your life would be built.

The Parents We Never Chose

Let's take a closer look at the people who brought us here: our parents. They weren't perfect. They came with their own baggage, shaped by their own upbringing, culture, and circumstances. These individuals, with their unique flaws and strengths, were chosen to be the vessels that brought you into existence.

You didn't choose your parents, and they didn't choose theirs. Yet their decisions, behaviors, and personalities played a significant role in shaping the person you would become. Some parents were loving and attentive, while others struggled to provide even the basics of care. Some were present, others absent. But one thing remains true for all of us: their actions—or inactions—left an imprint.

Traits, tendencies, and habits often run in families. You might have inherited your mother's stubbornness or your father's sense of humor. Or perhaps you've spent years trying to unlearn behaviors you picked up from them. Either way, the apple doesn't fall far from the tree—not because you're destined to become your parents, but because they were your first example of what life could or should look like.

A World Beyond Our Control

As a child, control wasn't in your vocabulary. Decisions were made for you: what you ate, where you lived, how you were raised. These decisions, made by your caregivers, shaped your perception of the world long before you were old enough to question them.

Some of us were born into stable, nurturing environments where love and support were abundant. Others faced chaos, neglect, or dysfunction. Regardless of where you fall on that spectrum, your experiences shaped your perspective, often in ways you didn't realize at the time.

Think about how this lack of control extended beyond your physical circumstances. You didn't get to choose the dynamics of your household, the personalities of the people around you, or even the emotional tone of your early life. Yet all these elements became part of the foundation upon which your identity was built.

The Power of the Mind

One of the greatest gifts God gave you is your mind. From the moment you entered this world, your brain began processing everything around you. Your conscious mind allowed you to observe and learn, but it's your subconscious mind that did the heavy lifting.

The subconscious mind is a remarkable creation, operating like a vast storage system that holds every experience, emotion, and memory you've ever encountered. Even things you don't consciously remember are stored there, quietly influencing your thoughts, habits, and behaviors.

For example, if you grew up in a home filled with love and encouragement, your subconscious mind likely recorded those experiences as a foundation of security. Conversely, if your environment was marked by conflict or instability, those experiences may have sown seeds of fear or mistrust.

9

What makes the subconscious mind so powerful is that it operates without you even realizing it. It's constantly at work, shaping your reactions, preferences, and beliefs based on the programming it received early in life. This is why two people can grow up in the same household yet interpret their experiences in completely different ways: their subconscious minds absorbed and processed the world uniquely.

The Weight of Early Programming

As a child, you didn't have the ability to filter what went into your subconscious mind. You absorbed everything, whether it was positive or negative. A loving parent who showered you with affection might have instilled a sense of self-worth. Meanwhile, a parent who was emotionally distant or critical could have unknowingly planted doubts about your value or ability to succeed.

These early experiences don't just shape your childhood; they carry over into adulthood, influencing how you approach relationships, challenges, and even your sense of self. Often, these influences operate so subtly that we don't recognize their origins until we take the time to reflect.

Welcome to the World

Here's the truth: the circumstances of your birth, the family you were born into, and the environment that shaped you weren't random. They were part of a plan, even if that plan doesn't always feel clear. The experiences you've had—both good and bad—have played a role in shaping the person you are today.

But while you couldn't control the beginning of your story, you do have the power to shape the rest of it. Your past doesn't define your future, and the patterns you absorbed in childhood don't have to dictate your life. The first step toward transformation is awareness: understanding where you came from and how those early experiences continue to influence you.

Shaping Relationships Through the Lens of the World

Now, let's bring this full circle into relationships, because this book is about more than just self-reflection; it's about understanding how your past influences the way you love and connect with others.

Everything you experienced when you were welcomed into this world—your family dynamics, your subconscious programming, the habits you picked up—becomes part of the "baggage" you bring into relationships. These patterns often surface in subtle ways, shaping how you communicate, how you handle conflict, and even how you express love.

For instance, if you grew up in a home where love was conditional, you might struggle to trust your partner's affection. If your childhood was marked by chaos, you might find yourself creating drama without realizing it because it feels "normal." On the other hand, if you were raised in an environment of stability and support, you might bring a sense of calm and reassurance into your relationships.

11

Understanding the roots of your behaviors is essential for building healthy connections. When two people come together in a relationship, they're not just bringing themselves—they're bringing their entire histories, their subconscious programming, and their unique worldviews. Recognizing this is the first step toward creating a partnership that is built on empathy, understanding, and mutual growth.

This book will guide you through the process of examining your "Welcome to the World" story and learning how it influences your relationships. By the end of this journey, you'll not only understand yourself better, but you'll also be equipped to navigate the complexities of love and connection with greater awareness and compassion.

So, welcome to the world. This is where your story began, but it's only the beginning of understanding how your past shapes your present and, ultimately, your relationships.

Exercises for Chapter 1: Welcome to the World

Exercise 1: Reflect and Share – "Your Childhood's Influence"

Prompt:

Identify three experiences from your childhood that you think help or hurt your relationship. Share these with your partner, explaining why you believe they have this effect. Then, invite your partner to share their experiences.

Why This Exercise Matters:

This activity encourages mutual understanding by helping both partners recognize how their early experiences shaped their relationship habits. It fosters empathy and creates a safe space to discuss vulnerabilities and strengths.

Exercise 2: Discussion – "The Parents We Never Chose"

Prompt:

Discuss how your parents' actions (or inactions) influenced your view of love, trust, and conflict. Use the following questions to guide your conversation:

- What is one positive lesson about relationships you learned from your parents?

- What is one thing you've had to unlearn from their example?
- How can we ensure we don't repeat harmful patterns from our families?

Why This Exercise Matters:

By examining the influence of parental models, couples can identify patterns they want to continue or break. This conversation lays the groundwork for building a healthier relationship together.

Exercise 3: Practical Action – "Identify Patterns"

Prompt:

Take time to individually reflect and list 3 subconscious patterns or behaviors you think you've carried from childhood into adulthood (e.g., avoiding conflict, people-pleasing, being overly critical). Discuss these with your partner, focusing on:

1. How these behaviors show up in your relationship.
2. Whether they help or hinder your connection.

Why This Exercise Matters:

This activity bridges self-awareness and communication. It helps couples become more intentional about recognizing patterns that need adjustment while providing an opportunity to support one another's growth.

Exercise 4: Goal-Setting – "Change One Pattern Together"

Prompt:

Choose one specific pattern or behavior that you both agree to work on together. For example:

- If one partner struggles with avoiding conflict, agree to address disagreements within 24 hours.
- If a partner is overly critical, commit to focusing on positive reinforcement at least once daily.

Write this goal down, agree on how to hold each other accountable, and check in weekly to measure progress.

Why This Exercise Matters:

This step transforms awareness into actionable growth. By setting a shared goal, couples learn to support one another in breaking unhelpful patterns while fostering accountability.

Scripture Reflection

Scripture:

"Do not conform to the pattern of this world but be transformed by the renewing of your mind. Then you will be able to test and approve what God's will is—his good, pleasing and perfect will." **(Romans 12:2)**

Takeaways:

1. **Awareness:** Reflect on the patterns you've carried from childhood and whether they align with God's will for your relationship.
2. **Transformation:** Renewing your mind requires intentional effort to change old habits that no longer serve you or your relationship.
3. **Unity in Growth:** As a couple, seek God's guidance in transforming your individual patterns into ones that strengthen your connection.

Goal for Chapter 1

Goal: Work together to identify one childhood pattern (for each partner) that you both agree to address or improve over the next month. Schedule weekly check-ins to celebrate progress and adjust strategies as needed.

Chapter 2

It's a Cold World

In Chapter 1, we talked about your early upbringing, your family influences, and the foundation that was laid during your earliest years. But now, imagine yourself as a young child, just beginning to step into the world beyond your home. Maybe you're 5 or 6 years old, heading off to school for the first time. It's here, outside the safety of your home environment, that you begin a new phase of life. You're now faced with the task of socializing, learning how to communicate, and navigating a whole new world of experiences.

This stage—from early childhood through your late teens—can completely reshape you. It's the time when the outside world begins to impose its rules, expectations, and challenges on you. You start to learn that the world isn't always kind, that not everyone is nice, and that some people don't have your best interests at heart.

For many of us, these years are filled with formative experiences, some as seemingly small as being teased on the playground, and others as significant as witnessing trauma in our neighborhoods or families. These experiences begin to shape how we see ourselves, others, and the world around us.

The Cold Reality of the World

When you first leave the safe cocoon of your family environment, you're introduced to the reality of the world. At school, you might encounter a child like Billy, the one who calls you names or pulls the girls' hair. If you grew up in a household where respect and kindness were emphasized, Billy's behavior might be shocking to you. You might wonder, "Why is he acting like this? Doesn't he know it's wrong?"

As you grow older, these interactions become more complex. Maybe you start noticing conflicts in the neighborhood—family altercations, substance abuse, or other troubling activities. These aren't just random events; they're shaping your understanding of the world and your place in it. They're teaching you lessons, whether consciously or subconsciously, about what's acceptable, what's dangerous, and how you should respond to challenges.

For some, these experiences can be traumatizing. Even something as seemingly small as being picked last for a team in gym class can stick with you. It can make you question your worth or ability to fit in. And as you continue to navigate life, you're constantly faced with decisions: Do I hold on to the values my parents taught me, or do I explore this new and unfamiliar behavior?

The Pressure to Conform

The world has a way of pushing its patterns on you. For instance, by the time you're in high school, you might encounter situations like Joey in the ninth grade, who brings drugs to school and offers them to you during lunch. He tells you, "This will make you feel good." In that moment, you're faced with a decision: Do I say no and risk being ridiculed, or do I give in and try it, even though I know it's wrong?

These moments of peer pressure aren't just about the immediate choice at hand—they're part of a larger process of shaping who you are. Every decision you make during these formative years is a response to the world around you. Whether you resist or conform, you're constantly learning about yourself and what you're capable of.

How This Shapes Your Relationships

Now, you might be wondering, "Allen, what does all of this have to do with my partner or the relationship I'm struggling with now?" The answer is simple: it has *everything* to do with it.

The world, from the earliest moments of your life, has been influencing how you think, feel, and behave. It has been teaching you how to respond to love, conflict, trust, and vulnerability. These lessons don't just disappear when you enter a relationship—they become the foundation upon which your partnership is built.

For instance, if your experiences in the world taught you that people can't be trusted, you might struggle to fully open up to your partner. If you've faced trauma or rejection, you might find it hard to believe that someone could truly love you without ulterior motives. On the flip side, if you grew up with strong values and a supportive network, you might enter relationships with a sense of stability and confidence.

But here's the catch: your partner has their own story. They've been shaped by their own unique experiences in the world, and those experiences may be vastly different from yours. This is where the potential for misunderstanding arises.

Withholding Judgment

One of the most important lessons you can take from this chapter is this: don't judge a person based solely on their actions or behaviors without considering the world they've come from. Everyone's experiences are different. What might seem irrational, hurtful, or confusing to you could be the result of trauma or lessons they learned during their formative years.

Let me share a personal example from my own life. I've been married for 27 years, and like any couple, my wife and I have had our ups and downs. Early in our relationship, while we were still in the courting stage, my wife asked me a question that initially offended me.

We were on a date, having a great time, and falling in love. Out of nowhere, she asked, "If you ever had daughters, would you harm them?"

I was stunned. My immediate reaction was anger. How could she even ask me such a thing? I thought, "What kind of person does she think I am?" I hadn't given her any reason to doubt my character, and the question felt like an attack.

But as I sat with the question, I realized it wasn't about me at all. It was about her past. Later, I learned that she had been violated as a child, and that experience had left her with deep scars. Her question wasn't an accusation—it was a way of protecting herself and trying to ensure her safety in our relationship.

This was a turning point for me. It taught me to look beyond my initial reaction and consider the world my wife had come from. Her experiences shaped her questions, her concerns, and her approach to our relationship.

The Impact of Broken Worlds

When you connect with someone, you're not just connecting with who they are today—you're connecting with everything that shaped them. Their childhood, their adolescence, their encounters with the world—all of these experiences come together to form their worldview.

If you want your relationship to succeed, you need to approach your partner with empathy and understanding. Recognize that their behaviors, even the ones that frustrate or confuse you, have roots in their past. Instead of judging them, ask questions. Seek to understand their story and how it has influenced them.

Moving Forward

This chapter is about recognizing the impact of the world on both you and your partner. The experiences you had growing up, the pressures you faced, and the lessons you learned all play a role in how you approach relationships.

As you continue reading, I encourage you to reflect on your own story and your partner's story. What challenges did you face as you found your place in the world? What lessons did you learn, and how are those lessons influencing your relationship today?

Remember, understanding is the key to connection. When you take the time to understand your partner's world, you're better equipped to navigate the complexities of love and build a relationship that can withstand the challenges of life.

Exercises for Chapter 2: It's a Cold World

Exercise 1: Reflect and Share – "The Cold Reality of the World"

Prompt:

Identify one key moment from your childhood or teen years that taught you something about trust, love, or conflict. Share this experience with your partner, explaining how it shaped the way you approach relationships today. Then, invite your partner to share a similar experience from their life.

Why This Exercise Matters:

This activity encourages vulnerability and mutual understanding. By sharing personal stories, couples can connect on a deeper level and begin to see how their partner's experiences shaped their behaviors and mindset.

Exercise 2: Discussion – "Understanding Pressure and Patterns"

Prompt:

Discuss how peer pressure or societal expectations influenced your decisions growing up. Use the following questions as a guide:

- What is one decision you regret due to outside influence?

- How do you think that decision impacts your approach to relationships now?
- What values or lessons did you learn about standing firm in your beliefs?

Why This Exercise Matters:

By examining how external pressures shaped them, couples can better understand their partner's struggles and strengths. This also opens a dialogue about shared values and boundaries.

Exercise 3: Practical Action – "Breaking the Judgment Cycle"

Prompt:

Both partners should identify one behavior or habit in the other that frustrates or confuses them. Instead of judging or criticizing, ask each other:

1. What life experience might have contributed to this behavior?
2. How can I support you in overcoming or managing this behavior?

Why This Exercise Matters:

This exercise fosters empathy and teamwork. By focusing on understanding rather than judgment, couples can transform frustration into compassion and growth.

Exercise 4: Goal-Setting – "Supporting Each Other's Growth"

Prompt:

Each partner should choose one area where they feel influenced by their past (e.g., avoiding vulnerability, overreacting to criticism). Together, create a shared plan to address these areas, such as:

- Setting aside time each week to discuss progress.
- Practicing specific techniques (e.g., active listening, affirmations).
- Agreeing to gently call each other out when old patterns resurface.

Why This Exercise Matters:

This goal-setting activity turns insight into action, helping couples actively work on growth areas while supporting each other in the process.

Scripture Reflection

Scripture:

"Can two walk together, except they be agreed?" (Amos 3:3)

Takeaways:

1. **Unity Requires Understanding**: Couples must strive for alignment in values, goals, and actions to walk the journey of life together effectively.

2. **Empathy Builds Agreement**: Understanding your partner's world fosters agreement and strengthens the bond between you.

3. **Intentional Effort**: True agreement doesn't happen by accident; it requires intentional, ongoing dialogue and effort.

Goal for Chapter 2

Goal:

Commit to having one in-depth conversation this week where each partner shares a story from their past that shaped their worldview. Focus on listening without judgment and finding ways to support each other in breaking any unhelpful patterns.

Chapter 3

The World Is Yours

After growing up and navigating your early experiences, you eventually reach a point in life where the restrictions of childhood and the rules of adolescence begin to fade. By the time you finish high school or transition into adulthood, a new phrase often emerges: The world is yours.

What does that mean? It means you've entered a stage where you are no longer bound by parental control or constant guidance. You're free to make your own choices, good or bad, and to pursue whatever you desire. For many, this milestone is exciting and full of promise, but it's also where significant challenges begin.

The World's Temptations

At this stage, you're exposed to even more of what the world offers—and not all of it is good. The Bible warns us in 1 John 2:16:

"For all that is in the world—the lust of the flesh, the lust of the eyes, and the pride of life—is not of the Father but is of the world." These three areas—lust, desire, and pride—are the primary tools Satan uses to pull us away from God's design.

The problem is that many of us at this stage don't fully understand what God requires of us or how He's trying to protect us from our own desires. We see the world as full of opportunity, yet we fail to realize how quickly our choices can lead to brokenness.

Freedom Without Guidance

When the world becomes yours, it's easy to think, "I can do what I want." But without the right guidance, this freedom can quickly lead to mistakes with lasting consequences. Many of us experience this in different ways:

1. Some engage in sexual activity before they're ready, leading to emotional or physical consequences, including unplanned pregnancies or sexually transmitted diseases.
2. Others are drawn into substance abuse, whether through experimentation or peer pressure.
3. Some make choices that conflict with their values, such as engaging in illegal activities or compromising their integrity for acceptance or gain.

At the time, these decisions might feel harmless or even empowering. But over time, the damage becomes clear. And for many, the mistakes made during this stage of life become baggage that they carry into future relationships.

My Personal Story

Let me share a personal example of how this played out in my own life. When I was 10 years old, I visited a friend's house. No one else was home, and my friend told me about some magazines hidden under the bed. Being curious, I checked them out. These weren't just magazines—they were pornographic materials, filled with images I'd never seen before.

At that age, I didn't fully understand what I was looking at, but I knew one thing: I liked it. That moment planted a seed in my mind—a strong desire to see more. I didn't realize it at the time, but this exposure would shape how I viewed women and relationships for years to come.

As I got older, that initial exposure to pornography didn't fade away. By the time I was in my teenage years, my friends and I would gather to watch explicit videos. We didn't see it as harmful; it was just something we did. But these experiences were slowly distorting my understanding of women, relationships, and intimacy.

Fast forward to adulthood, when the world was mine. I was free to do what I wanted without answering to my parents. One of the choices I made during this time was to frequent strip clubs. I didn't realize it then, but this behavior was giving me a false sense of what a relationship with a woman should be. It was shaping my expectations in ways that were neither healthy nor realistic.

The Damage of False Narratives

Looking back, I see how these early exposures affected me. The pornography, the strip clubs—they created a narrative in my mind that was far from God's design for love and relationships. They taught me to view women as objects rather than as partners, and that mindset caused damage I didn't fully understand until much later in life.

This is the danger of the world being "yours." Without proper guidance, the choices you make during this stage can lead to brokenness that carries over into every aspect of your life—including your relationships.

Lust, Pride, and Brokenness

The Bible's warning about the lust of the flesh, the lust of the eyes, and the pride of life is crucial here because these are the areas where most of us struggle when the world becomes ours.

- **Lust of the Flesh:** This can take many forms—sexual temptation, overindulgence, or a focus on physical gratification. For me, it was the early exposure to pornography and the later pursuit of physical experiences that left me spiritually and emotionally drained.

- **Lust of the Eyes:** This is the desire for things that are visually appealing but ultimately harmful. It's the allure of materialism, envy, or coveting what others have.

- **The Pride of Life:** This is the most subtle of the three but often the most destructive. Pride can lead us to reject correction, refuse to seek help, or prioritize our ego over our relationships.

All of these temptations are designed to pull us away from God and leave us broken. And when we're broken, it becomes difficult to form healthy, lasting relationships.

How This Affects Relationships

When you enter into a relationship, you bring everything you've experienced in the world with you—the good, the bad, and the unresolved. For example, someone who struggled with sexual temptation might find it hard to establish trust and intimacy in a relationship. Someone who battled with pride might struggle to admit fault or compromise.

What's important to understand is that everyone carries some level of brokenness into their relationships. Some wounds are small and manageable, while others are deep and significant. The key is to recognize these wounds, address them, and strive for healing.

Additional Examples

Let's consider some other scenarios:

A young woman grows up in an environment where materialism is emphasized. When she enters adulthood, she believes her worth is tied to how she looks or what she owns. This mindset carries over into her relationships, leading to conflict or insecurity.

A young man is introduced to drugs during his teenage years. By the time he enters a relationship, he's battling addiction, which creates strain and distrust between him and his partner.

In both cases, the choices made when the world was "theirs" continue to impact their ability to build healthy, meaningful relationships.

Moving Forward

At this stage of life, many of us look back on the decisions we've made and wish we could change them. But dwelling on past mistakes won't help us move forward. Instead, we need to focus on learning from those experiences and making better choices moving forward.

The world may have been yours, but that doesn't mean it has to define you. God's grace is bigger than any mistake you've made, and His plan for you includes healing, restoration, and growth.

As you reflect on this chapter, think about how your choices during this stage of life have shaped your relationships. Are there patterns or behaviors you need to address? Are there wounds you need to heal? By acknowledging these areas, you can begin to break free from the past and move toward the healthy, God-centered relationships you were designed to have.

Exercises for Chapter 3: The World Is Yours

Exercise 1: Reflect and Share – "Choices and Their Consequences"

Prompt: Identify one decision you made when "the world became yours" that has impacted your relationships. Reflect on whether this decision helped or hurt you, and share your experience with your partner. Then, ask your partner to share a similar story from their life.

Why This Exercise Matters:

By reflecting on past decisions, couples can better understand how their individual choices shaped their current behaviors and mindsets. Sharing these stories fosters empathy and opens the door for meaningful conversations about growth and healing.

Exercise 2: Discussion – "The Impact of Temptations"

Prompt: As a couple, discuss how the "lust of the flesh, the lust of the eyes, and the pride of life" (1 John 2:16) have affected your individual lives or relationship. Use these questions to guide your conversation:

- Which of these areas do you struggle with the most?

- How has this struggle influenced your relationship?
- What steps can you take together to address these challenges?

Why This Exercise Matters:

This discussion helps couples recognize the spiritual and emotional impact of temptations while encouraging them to support each other in overcoming these struggles.

Exercise 3: Practical Action – "Breaking False Narratives"

Prompt: Individually, write down one false narrative or belief you've carried from past experiences (e.g., "I need to be perfect to be loved" or "Relationships always end in pain"). Share this with your partner and discuss:

1. How this belief started.
2. How it influences your relationship.
3. What steps you both can take to replace this narrative with truth.

Why This Exercise Matters:

This exercise promotes self-awareness and creates a pathway for couples to replace unhealthy beliefs with truths that align with love, respect, and faith.

Exercise 4: Goal-Setting – "Building a New World Together"

Prompt: Create a shared goal that helps you both grow in one of the areas discussed in this chapter (e.g., resisting temptations, addressing past wounds, or breaking unhealthy patterns). Examples of goals:

1. Commit to weekly check-ins about personal struggles and spiritual growth.
2. Replace an unhealthy habit with a shared activity, like exercising or praying together.

Why This Exercise Matters:

Goal-setting as a couple reinforces unity and creates accountability. It also helps partners focus on building a future together, free from the baggage of past mistakes.

Scripture Reflection

Scripture:

"For all that is in the world—the lust of the flesh, the lust of the eyes, and the pride of life—is not of the Father but is of the world." **(1 John 2:16)**

Takeaways:

1. **Recognize Temptations:** Be mindful of how the world's temptations can distract from God's purpose for your relationship.

2. **Seek God's Guidance:** Overcoming lust, pride, or unhealthy desires requires relying on God's strength, not just your own willpower.

3. **Encourage Accountability:** As a couple, commit to supporting each other in resisting temptations and pursuing God's plan for your relationship.

Goal for Chapter 3

Goal: Identify one area where past temptations or choices continue to affect your relationship. Create a plan to address it together, such as setting boundaries, replacing unhealthy habits, or seeking counseling or spiritual support.

Chapter 4

Exploring New Worlds

As you can see from the last chapter, life has a way of shaping us through the experiences we endure and the choices we make. Many of these choices, especially when the world becomes "ours," can leave us with scars that we don't always see right away. These scars often emerge later, particularly when we decide to enter relationships. This chapter, **Exploring New Worlds**, is the perfect opportunity to dive into the dynamics of dating and connecting with another person's world.

By now, you've experienced enough of life to have formed your own habits, beliefs, and coping mechanisms. These patterns often come from early exposure to the world's temptations or even harmful lessons we've learned along the way. For me personally, as I shared in the last chapter, the habits and mindsets I developed in my younger years influenced how I viewed relationships and the opposite gender. These early experiences didn't just fade away; they followed me into adulthood, sometimes hindering my ability to have healthy connections.

The Weight of Comparisons

One of the greatest challenges many people face when entering a relationship is the tendency to compare. Whether consciously or subconsciously, we measure our current experiences against past ones. This is one of the dangers of being exposed to things like pornography, casual relationships, or unhealthy dynamics early in life. These experiences set a precedent in your mind, and you begin to make comparisons—often unfair ones—when you're with a new partner.

For example, let's say you're in a relationship, and your partner doesn't meet a standard you've developed based on past experiences. Maybe someone from your past excelled in a certain area, and now you expect the same or better from your current partner. The problem with this mindset is that it reduces people to performances, ignoring the deeper, emotional connection that relationships require.

This is one reason the Bible encourages us to avoid certain behaviors and choices before marriage. God's design is intended to protect us from the baggage and brokenness that often come with these comparisons. Unfortunately, many of us don't realize this wisdom until we've already been hurt or caused harm in relationships.

38

Two Worlds Colliding

When you decide to enter a relationship, you're not just bringing your present self—you're bringing your entire world with you. Your world consists of everything you've experienced, from your childhood upbringing to the lessons life has taught you. But here's the challenge: the person you're connecting with also has their own world.

When two worlds come together, it's not always a perfect fit. Each person has their own perspectives, desires, and ways of coping with life's challenges. Often, these differences can create friction. For example, one person might come from a background where they were taught to avoid conflict at all costs, while the other grew up in a household where disagreements were loud and frequent. These two approaches to conflict resolution can clash, leading to misunderstandings and frustration.

The truth is, most people don't show the full reality of their world right away. When we first meet someone, we tend to highlight the best parts of ourselves—the shiny, polished aspects of our personality that we think will attract the other person. We leave the broken, messy parts hidden in the shadows.

But over time, as the relationship deepens, those hidden parts inevitably surface. The secrets, traumas, and unresolved issues from each person's world come to light, and they can create significant challenges in the relationship.

The Importance of Understanding

One of the keys to navigating the collision of two worlds is understanding. It's important to recognize that everyone brings baggage into a relationship. Some of this baggage is light and manageable, while some of it is heavy and deeply rooted. Either way, it's crucial to approach your partner with empathy and a willingness to understand their story.

For example, one partner may have limited exposure to sexuality, while the other has experienced it extensively. These differences can create discomfort or even incompatibility if not handled with care. It's important to have open, honest conversations about each person's background, expectations, and values. Without these conversations, misunderstandings can fester and lead to resentment.

Loving Through Brokenness

Every world has broken pieces. Whether it's past relationships, childhood trauma, or societal pressures, we all carry scars that affect how we interact with others. When two broken worlds come together, the cracks and imperfections often become more apparent.

But here's the beauty of love: it has the power to transcend brokenness. Once you've made a commitment to someone, it's up to both of you to work together to create a new world—a shared world—where healing and growth can take place. This doesn't mean ignoring or dismissing the broken parts of your partner's world. Instead, it means learning to love them despite those imperfections.

In my own marriage, I've had to confront my own shortcomings and learn to love my wife through hers. One of the challenges I faced early on was my tendency to make comparisons. Because of the things I was exposed to in my younger years, I sometimes found myself unfairly measuring my wife against unrealistic expectations. This wasn't her fault—it was a result of my own brokenness.

Over time, I realized that true love requires humility and self-reflection. It's not about finding someone who fits perfectly into your world; it's about building a new world together, piece by piece.

The Danger of Hiding

One of the biggest obstacles to building a healthy relationship is the tendency to hide. As I mentioned earlier, many people present only the best parts of their world, keeping the messy, broken parts hidden. This might work in the beginning, but eventually, those hidden parts will come to the surface.

For example, someone might enter a relationship without revealing past traumas, financial struggles, or unresolved issues. They might think they're protecting the relationship by keeping these things hidden, but in reality, they're creating a foundation of secrecy and mistrust.

The only way to truly connect with someone is to be open and honest about your world, even the parts you're not proud of. This doesn't mean dumping all your baggage on the table at once, but it does mean being willing to share your story and let your partner into your world.

Building a New World Together

When two worlds come together, there will always be challenges. But with patience, communication, and a commitment to growth, it's possible to create a new world that reflects the best of both people. This new world won't be perfect—it will still have its flaws and struggles—but it will be built on a foundation of mutual understanding and love.

As you reflect on this chapter, I encourage you to think about your own world and the world of your partner. What are the hidden pieces that need to be addressed? What are the strengths and weaknesses that you bring to the relationship? And most importantly, how can you work together to create a new world that is stronger, healthier, and more loving than either world on its own?

Exercises for Chapter 4: Exploring New Worlds

Exercise 1: Reflect and Share – "What's in Your World?"

Prompt: Individually reflect on the "hidden parts" of your world—experiences, habits, or beliefs that you may not have fully shared with your partner. Choose one or two to discuss openly, answering these questions:

- How has this part of your world influenced who you are today?
- How do you think it impacts your relationship?

Encourage your partner to share as well, creating a safe space for mutual understanding.

Why This Exercise Matters:

This activity builds trust and vulnerability. By sharing the less-visible parts of your world, you and your partner can deepen your connection and navigate challenges together with empathy and awareness.

Exercise 2: Discussion – "Two Worlds Colliding"

Prompt: Sit down with your partner and talk about moments when your "worlds" have clashed. Use the following questions to guide your conversation:

- What's one area where we've had a conflict because of our different upbringings or experiences?
- How can we better approach these differences in the future?
- What can we learn from each other's perspective?

Why This Exercise Matters:

This discussion helps couples identify and address points of friction in their relationship. It encourages problem-solving and promotes understanding of how each person's unique background contributes to conflicts.

Exercise 3: Practical Action – "Breaking the Cycle of Comparison"

Prompt: Reflect on whether comparisons—conscious or subconscious—have influenced your relationship. As a couple, identify one or two ways you can replace comparison with gratitude. For example:

- Instead of comparing your partner to someone from your past, identify three qualities you love about them today.
- Focus on building each other up with affirmations rather than dwelling on past experiences.

Why This Exercise Matters:

This exercise helps couples move away from harmful comparisons and toward appreciation. It fosters a culture of encouragement and positivity within the relationship.

Exercise 4: Goal-Setting – "Creating a Shared World"

Prompt: Discuss one specific area where your "worlds" can be combined to create a stronger partnership. Examples include:

• Establishing new traditions together (e.g., weekly date nights or family rituals).

• Setting joint goals for personal growth, finances, or spiritual connection.

Write down your shared goal, outline steps to achieve it, and agree to check in regularly on your progress.

Why This Exercise Matters:

This goal-setting exercise emphasizes collaboration and the importance of building a unified world. It encourages couples to focus on creating a future that reflects their shared values and aspirations.

Scripture Reflection

Scripture: "Love is patient, love is kind. It does not envy, it does not boast, it is not proud. It does not dishonor others, it is not self-seeking, it is not easily angered, it keeps no record of wrongs." **(1 Corinthians 13:4-5)**

Takeaways:

1. **Patience and Kindness:** Love grows when both partners approach each other's world with gentleness and understanding.

2. **Selflessness:** Building a shared world requires setting aside ego and focusing on the needs of the relationship.

3. **Forgiveness:** To navigate differences, couples must let go of past hurts and choose to move forward together.

Goal for Chapter 4

Goal: Work together to identify one "hidden" part of each other's world that hasn't been fully explored. Create a plan to address this openly and positively, focusing on building trust and strengthening your bond.

Chapter 5

Creating a New World

After spending time dating, learning about each other, and possibly going through an engagement period, there comes a pivotal point in many relationships where you decide to commit fully. This commitment, often symbolized by marriage, is the merging of two worlds into one—a process that is both beautiful and challenging.

For me, this moment came early in my relationship with my wife. Just a few days after meeting her, I knew I wanted to marry her, and we were engaged shortly after. A year later, we tied the knot. Even at that time, there were still many things we didn't fully know about each other's worlds. But we made the decision to bring our worlds together and create a new one—a world we would share as husband and wife.

The Commitment to Cleave

The Bible says in **Genesis 2:24**, *"Therefore a man shall leave his father and mother and be joined to his wife, and they shall become one flesh."* This concept of "cleaving together" represents the deep union that happens when two lives are joined. But this is not just a physical or legal joining; it's the coming together of two entirely different worlds—worlds that may have been shaped by different values, experiences, and even traumas.

Bringing two worlds together is not easy. It's not just about sharing a home or a name; it's about blending two lives into one harmonious partnership. Each world comes with its own unique set of desires, ambitions, brokenness, and habits. The process of merging these worlds requires patience, humility, and an understanding that not everything will change—or needs to.

Accepting Each Other's Brokenness

One of the things I quickly discovered after marrying my wife was that there were aspects of her world that were deeply affected by her past. She had experienced trauma at an early age, which altered her sense of what was normal and created challenges in our relationship. Trauma affects everyone differently, and for my wife, it manifested in ways that were sometimes difficult for me to understand or deal with.

There were moments of frustration where I didn't know how to handle her pain or her responses to certain situations. But what I learned over time is that patience is key. In a committed relationship,

48

you must accept that there will be challenges—some you can address, and others you simply have to navigate with love and grace.

Communication and Understanding

If your relationship is going to last, one of the most important things you need is *understanding*. The Bible emphasizes this in **Proverbs 4:7**: *"Wisdom is the principal thing; therefore get wisdom: and with all thy getting get understanding."*

Understanding is the ability to truly comprehend your partner's feelings, experiences, and perspective. Without it, many problems in a relationship can persist for years, simply because they're not fully communicated or understood.

For example, some couples may never agree on certain topics, such as political views or personal habits. But disagreement doesn't have to lead to division. Love, when rooted in understanding, allows you to accept your partner's differences without letting them undermine the foundation of your relationship.

The Danger of Independence in Unity

In today's world, many couples struggle with the idea of truly becoming one. While they may unite symbolically through marriage, they continue to operate as separate individuals—holding onto their independence rather than embracing the partnership.

This mindset can be disastrous. Marriage requires a shift in focus, where the "me" becomes "we." When two people refuse to merge their lives, goals, and efforts, it creates division and makes it difficult to move forward together.

The Bible says in **Amos 3:3**, *"Can two walk together, except they be agreed?"* Agreement is a cornerstone of any successful relationship. Without it, you'll find yourselves at a standstill, unable to progress because your goals and visions aren't aligned.

The Power of Agreement

Agreement doesn't mean that you and your partner will always see eye-to-eye on every issue. It means that you're committed to finding common ground and working together toward a shared goal. It requires compromise, open communication, and a willingness to prioritize the relationship over individual preferences.

For example, if one partner wants to pursue a career path that requires relocation, but the other partner is hesitant to leave their current environment, it's essential to have honest conversations about how to move forward. The goal isn't for one person to "win" the argument but to find a solution that honors both perspectives.

Building Peace Through Understanding

One of the greatest gifts you can give your partner—and your relationship—is the acknowledgment that no one is perfect. Everyone enters a relationship with flaws, past experiences, and areas of brokenness. Accepting this reality creates space for patience, empathy, and peace.

As we learn from **Proverbs 4:7**, understanding is essential. Understanding doesn't just mean hearing your partner's words; it means truly listening, seeking to comprehend their perspective, and responding with love and grace.

When you approach your relationship with this mindset, challenges become opportunities for growth rather than obstacles. You begin to see your partner not as someone who needs to be fixed but as someone who is worthy of love and support, even in their imperfections.

The Journey of Creating a New World

Creating a new world with your partner is a journey, not a destination. It's a process that requires ongoing effort, patience, and commitment. There will be moments of joy and moments of frustration, but through it all, the goal is to build a life together that reflects the best of both worlds.

Remember, the decision to marry or commit to someone is not just about love; it's about choosing to walk through life together, supporting each other through the ups and downs. It's about merging two worlds into one unified partnership, where both individuals are valued, understood, and loved.

As you reflect on this chapter, ask yourself:

- How can I better understand my partner's world?
- What areas of my own world need healing or growth?
- How can we work together to create a new world that reflects the love, patience, and unity God intended?

The journey won't always be easy, but with faith, understanding, and a commitment to cleaving together as one, it's a journey worth taking.

Exercises for Chapter 5: Creating a New World

Exercise 1: Reflect and Share – "Understanding Each Other's Brokenness"

Prompt: Each partner should take time to reflect on one area of their past that they believe has shaped their relationship—positively or negatively. Share this with each other, answering these questions:

- How does this part of your world influence your relationship today?

- What support or understanding do you need from your partner regarding this part of your past?

Why This Exercise Matters:

This activity fosters vulnerability and empathy by encouraging partners to open up about the parts of their world that might still impact their relationship. It creates an opportunity for healing and connection.

Exercise 2: Discussion – "The Power of Agreement"

Prompt: Sit down together and discuss one area where your visions or goals differ. Use these questions to guide your conversation:

- What is the root of each person's perspective on this issue?
- What compromises can be made to find common ground?
- How can we ensure our decision strengthens our partnership rather than creating division?

Why This Exercise Matters:

This discussion teaches couples how to navigate disagreements constructively, emphasizing the importance of finding solutions that honor both perspectives while strengthening unity.

Exercise 3: Practical Action – "Merging Our Lives"

Prompt: Choose one practical way to further merge your worlds this week. This could include:

- Creating a shared budget or financial plan.
- Establishing a weekly routine or tradition together (e.g., Sunday dinners or nightly walks).
- Collaborating on a home project or activity that reflects your combined interests.

Why This Exercise Matters:

This exercise reinforces the idea that marriage or commitment is about building a shared life. By taking actionable steps to combine your efforts, you actively create a new world together.

Exercise 4: Goal-Setting – "Cleaving Together"

Prompt: Set one relationship goal that aligns with the idea of "cleaving together." Examples include:

- Commit to resolving disagreements before the end of the day, as advised in Ephesians 4:26 ("Do not let the sun go down on your anger").
- Attend a couple's class, seminar, or counseling session to strengthen your understanding of each other.
- Begin a joint spiritual practice, like praying together daily or studying a passage of scripture weekly.

Why This Exercise Matters:

Goal-setting as a couple encourages unity, collaboration, and intentionality in the relationship. It helps partners focus on building a foundation of love, understanding, and shared growth.

Scripture Reflection

Scripture: "Therefore a man shall leave his father and mother and be joined to his wife, and they shall become one flesh." (Genesis 2:24)

Takeaways:

1. **Unity:** Marriage or commitment is about becoming one in purpose, vision, and love, not just in name or formality.
2. **Separation for Connection:** Leaving behind past dependencies is essential for fully embracing the partnership.
3. **Building Together:** True unity requires intentional effort to merge lives, heal brokenness, and work toward shared goals.

Goal for Chapter 5

Goal: Identify one area where you and your partner can better align your goals, values, or habits. Create an action plan together to address this area, and commit to checking in on your progress weekly.

Chapter 6

When Worlds Collide

As a married couple in a committed relationship, I can say that my wife and I have experienced our share of ups and downs. Over the course of our 27-year relationship, there were moments where the brokenness in each of us revealed itself in ways we didn't anticipate. These weren't fleeting difficulties; they were real, often challenging moments that tested the strength of our commitment.

This chapter is about those moments—when two worlds collide. When two people, shaped by different experiences and perspectives, come together, friction is inevitable. It's not just a clash of personalities; it's often the result of deep-seated habits, beliefs, and brokenness that resurface during conflict. The question is, how do we navigate these collisions and emerge stronger on the other side?

The Impact of Brokenness

My wife grew up in a single-parent household and didn't have the opportunity to see how a mother and father interact in the home. I, on the other hand, was raised in a two-parent household where I saw my father model certain behaviors toward my mother and the other way around. Naturally, I carried expectations into our marriage based on what I had witnessed growing up.

These expectations often clashed with my wife's reality. What I considered "normal" was foreign to her. For example, I expected attentiveness in specific ways because I had seen my mother demonstrate this in her relationship with my father. But for my wife, who hadn't seen that dynamic, those actions didn't come naturally.

This created tension in our relationship in the beginning. At times, I found myself frustrated, not understanding why she didn't meet my expectations. But over time, I realized it wasn't a lack of love or care on her part—it was simply a difference in how our worlds had been shaped and what was not natural for her at that time..

Learning How to Argue

When my wife and I had our first argument, it exposed a significant difference in how we viewed and handled conflict. For her, arguments felt final. She saw them as a sign that the relationship was in trouble—an experience rooted in her past where conflict often led to separation or disconnection.

On the other hand, I viewed arguments as a way to find solutions. From my perspective, disagreements were part of a healthy relationship—a way to air out issues and work toward resolution. To me, the argument wasn't the end; it was a necessary step to create understanding.

This difference created early tension in our marriage. My wife would shut down, thinking the relationship was on the brink, while I was still actively trying to address the problem. I had to reassure her that our arguments weren't signs of failure but opportunities to grow closer.

If there are arguments in your relationship, it's important to have a clear goal in mind: work toward a solution. Arguments should not be about assigning blame or venting frustrations with no direction. Instead, use them as opportunities to understand each other better and to address the root causes of the disagreement. Always argue with a purpose, focusing on resolving the issue and strengthening the relationship rather than tearing it down.

Navigating Collisions

When two worlds collide, the immediate instinct might be to withdraw, argue, or blame. But these reactions often escalate the conflict rather than resolving it. To navigate these moments effectively, it's important to approach them with patience, empathy, and a willingness to adapt.

Here are some strategies for handling conflict when worlds collide:

1. **Pause Before Reacting**

   In the heat of the moment, emotions can cloud judgment. Taking a step back to process your thoughts and emotions can prevent unnecessary escalation. This doesn't mean ignoring the issue—it means creating space to approach it with clarity.

2. **Be Specific About the Issue**

   One of the biggest pitfalls in conflict is generalization. Avoid making statements like, "You always do this," or "You never understand me." Instead, focus on the specific behavior or situation causing tension and discuss it constructively.

3. **Recognize the Root Cause**

   Often, the immediate argument isn't about what it seems on the surface. For example, a disagreement about household chores might actually be about feeling unappreciated. Take time to identify the underlying issue and address it directly.

4. **Seek Solutions, Not Victories**

   In a healthy relationship, the goal of conflict resolution isn't to "win" the argument but to strengthen the partnership. Shift your focus from proving a point to finding a solution that works for both of you.

5. **Take Breaks When Needed**

   If a conversation becomes too heated, it's okay to pause and revisit it later. Stepping away can give both parties time to cool off and reflect, making it easier to approach the issue with a fresh perspective.

The Danger of Unrealistic Expectations

One of the most common sources of conflict is unmet expectations. When we enter a relationship, we often carry assumptions about how things should be—assumptions based on our own upbringing and experiences.

For example, I assumed that my wife would naturally exhibit certain behaviors I had seen in my parents' relationship. But when she didn't, I felt disappointed and frustrated. What I failed to recognize at first was that my expectations were based on my world, not hers.

Unrealistic expectations can create resentment and strain in a relationship. The key is to communicate your needs and desires openly while also being willing to adapt and compromise.

Choosing Commitment Over Convenience

In today's world, it's easy to throw in the towel when conflicts arise. We're constantly bombarded with the idea that there's someone else out there who will meet all our needs without conflict. But the truth is, every person comes with their own set of challenges and imperfections.

Leaving one relationship to find another doesn't eliminate brokenness—it simply shifts the focus to a new set of issues. Commitment means choosing to stay and work through the difficulties, even when it's uncomfortable. It means recognizing that the grass isn't always greener on the other side and that true growth comes from nurturing the relationship you're in.

Building Bridges Instead of Walls

When worlds collide, the temptation is often to build walls—to protect yourself from further hurt or frustration. But building walls only creates distance and prevents the relationship from growing. Instead, focus on building bridges—ways to connect and understand each other better.

For example:

- **Ask Open-Ended Questions:** Instead of assuming you know why your partner feels a certain way, ask them to explain. This shows that you value their perspective and want to understand.
- **Express Vulnerability:** Sharing your own fears, insecurities, and struggles can create a safe space for your partner to do the same.
- **Focus on Common Goals:** Remind yourselves of the shared vision you have for your relationship and use that as motivation to work through challenges.

Moving Forward

When two worlds collide, it's not a sign that the relationship is failing—it's a natural part of two people learning to live and grow together. These moments of tension are opportunities to deepen your understanding of each other and strengthen your bond.

As you navigate conflicts, remember:

- Every person brings brokenness into a relationship.
- Conflict isn't about winning; it's about finding solutions together.
- Patience, empathy, and communication are key to resolving tensions.

Instead of seeing collisions as obstacles, view them as opportunities to create a stronger, more unified world. With commitment, understanding, and a willingness to grow, you can turn even the most challenging moments into stepping stones toward a healthier, happier relationship.

Exercises for Chapter 6: When Worlds Collide

Exercise 1: Reflect and Share – "The Root of the Collision"

Prompt: Think about a recent conflict in your relationship where you felt frustrated or misunderstood. Reflect on the deeper issue behind the conflict. Share with your partner:

- What triggered your reaction?
- What deeper emotion or unmet need might have contributed to how you responded?
- Then, listen as your partner shares their perspective on the same conflict.

Why This Exercise Matters: This activity encourages both partners to move beyond surface-level arguments and identify the root causes of their conflicts. By doing so, they can address the real issues rather than the symptoms.

Exercise 2: Practical Action – "Resetting Expectations"

Prompt: Each partner should identify one expectation they have of the other that might be rooted in their own upbringing or past experiences (e.g., "I expect you to handle conflict like my parents did" or "I expect you to express love the way I was taught love looks like"). Share these expectations and discuss:

1. Whether they are realistic.
2. How these expectations might create tension.
3. How you can adjust or better communicate them moving forward.

Why This Exercise Matters: Unmet or unrealistic expectations often lead to frustration. This exercise promotes open communication and helps couples realign their expectations with mutual understanding.

Exercise 3: Discussion – "Building Bridges, Not Walls"

Prompt: Work together to brainstorm three specific ways you can build "bridges" in your relationship rather than "walls" during moments of conflict. For example:

- Practicing active listening without interrupting.
- Taking a walk together during heated discussions to create physical movement while talking.
- Establishing a "time-out" system when arguments escalate, followed by a set time to revisit the issue.

Why This Exercise Matters: This exercise equips couples with actionable strategies to stay connected and avoid building emotional barriers during difficult moments.

Exercise 4: Goal-Setting – "Commitment Over Convenience"

Prompt: As a couple, create a shared commitment statement about how you will approach conflicts moving forward. Include:

- A mutual promise to address issues without walking away.

- A plan for how to handle heated moments (e.g., taking breaks, seeking help, praying together).
- A reminder of your shared vision and goals as a couple.

Why This Exercise Matters: A commitment statement provides a clear framework for handling conflicts in a way that prioritizes growth and unity. It reinforces the importance of choosing commitment over convenience.

Scripture Reflection

Scripture: "Bear with each other and forgive one another if any of you has a grievance against someone. Forgive as the Lord forgave you." **(Colossians 3:13)**

Takeaways:

1. **Patience in Conflict:** Relationships thrive when both partners are willing to bear with one another, even in moments of tension.
2. **The Power of Forgiveness:** Resolving conflicts often requires letting go of resentment and choosing to forgive.
3. **Modeling Grace:** Embracing forgiveness reflects God's grace and strengthens the bond between partners.

Goal for Chapter 6

Goal: Identify one recurring conflict in your relationship and create a shared plan for how to address it constructively moving forward. Commit to revisiting and refining this plan as needed.

Chapter 7

Changing Your World One Goal at a Time

When two worlds come together, as we've discussed in previous chapters, they bring their strengths, challenges, and brokenness. But while it's important to understand and navigate the dynamics of your shared world with your partner, it's equally important to focus on your individual world. *Changing the world one goal at a time* begins with you.

Self-awareness is critical in any relationship. Even if your partner has areas of brokenness or struggles, your ability to improve yourself and set meaningful goals will not only strengthen your world but also add value to your relationship. Far too often, people become complacent in their personal growth, assuming the responsibilities of the relationship will sort themselves out. But a stagnant world is a world at risk of falling apart.

The Importance of Self-Education

One of the most powerful ways to set goals for yourself is through self-education. Many people stop learning once they leave school, but education shouldn't end there—especially when it comes to relationships. There is a wealth of knowledge available about communication, conflict resolution, love languages, and understanding a partner's emotional needs.

For example, if you're in a relationship with someone who struggles with emotional expression due to past trauma, it would be wise to educate yourself on how to navigate those waters. Instead of getting frustrated or giving up, research ways to provide a safe environment for your partner. Learn about the impact of trauma and how patience and empathy can create a space for healing.

Self-education isn't just about books and articles—it's also about observing your partner and taking note of what makes them feel valued, loved, and understood. When you set a goal to learn more about the person you're with, you're not only improving yourself but also strengthening your connection.

Setting Goals for Self-Improvement

Every world has room for improvement, and that includes yours. Setting goals for yourself is one of the most effective ways to ensure you're growing as an individual and contributing positively to your relationship. These goals can focus on different areas of your life, including:

1. **Mental Goals**

   Challenge yourself to develop a healthier mindset. If you find yourself getting into frequent arguments, set a goal to pause and think before reacting. Practice mindfulness or journaling to reflect on your emotions and responses.

2. **Spiritual Goals**

   Growth isn't just about the physical or mental—it's about the spiritual as well. Feed yourself spiritually by spending time in prayer, reading scripture, or engaging in activities that strengthen your faith. The Bible reminds us to *"grow in the grace and knowledge of our Lord and Savior Jesus Christ"* (2 Peter 3:18). Spiritual growth gives you the strength to face challenges with a sense of peace and direction.

3. **Emotional Goals**

   Relationships require emotional intelligence. Set a goal to actively listen during conversations, practice empathy, and express your feelings in a way that fosters understanding rather than conflict.

4. **Relational Goals**

   Even within your relationship, you can set goals to become a better partner. This might mean planning intentional date nights, working on better communication, or learning your partner's love language and making an effort to express love in the way they best receive it.

71

The Power of Small, Achievable Goals

Change doesn't happen overnight, and that's okay. Start small. If you know you struggle with patience, set a goal to take a deep breath and count to ten before responding in moments of frustration. If you want to grow spiritually, commit to reading one scripture a day or attending a weekly Bible study.

Small goals lead to big changes. Over time, these small steps will accumulate, and you'll find that your world is shifting in ways you never thought possible.

Growing Together

The beauty of working on yourself is that it naturally impacts your relationship in positive ways. When you focus on becoming a better version of yourself, your partner benefits as well. You become more patient, understanding, and intentional, which creates a stronger foundation for your shared world.

Setting goals isn't about trying to fix yourself or your partner; it's about striving to grow and evolve so that your relationship has the best chance of thriving. A healthy relationship starts with healthy individuals, and that begins with a commitment to change your world one goal at a time.

Exercises for Chapter 7: Changing Your World One Goal at a Time

Exercise 1: Reflect and Share – "Your Personal Goals"

Prompt: Individually reflect on one personal goal that would help you grow as a person and positively impact your relationship. Share this goal with your partner, answering these questions:

- Why is this goal important to you?
- How do you think achieving this goal will benefit your relationship?
- What support, if any, do you need from your partner to achieve this goal?

Why This Exercise Matters: This activity encourages self-awareness and opens a dialogue about how individual growth contributes to the strength of the relationship. It fosters mutual support and accountability.

Exercise 2: Discussion – "Shared Learning"

Prompt: Choose a topic related to relationships (e.g., communication, conflict resolution, love languages) and commit to learning about it together. Discuss:

- What topic would help us grow as a couple?

- How will we explore this topic (e.g., reading a book, attending a seminar, or watching a video)?

- What insights can we apply to improve our relationship?

Why This Exercise Matters: This exercise highlights the value of shared education. It strengthens the partnership by encouraging both partners to actively invest in their relationship.

Exercise 3: Practical Action – "One Small Step"

Prompt: Individually, set one small, actionable goal that you can work on this week to improve yourself or your relationship. Examples include:

- Practicing active listening during conversations.

- Starting or ending each day with a moment of gratitude for your partner.

- Taking time to pray or meditate to strengthen your mental and spiritual focus.

At the end of the week, check in with each other to discuss how these small steps impacted your relationship.

Why This Exercise Matters: This exercise emphasizes the power of small changes and their cumulative effect on personal growth and the relationship.

Exercise 4: Goal-Setting – "Growth Together"

Prompt: As a couple, set a shared goal that supports mutual growth. This could include:

- Committing to a regular date night or quality time each week.

- Creating a plan to support each other's personal goals.

- Developing a joint spiritual practice, such as praying together or attending a faith-based event.

Write down this shared goal, and outline three steps you'll take to achieve it.

Why This Exercise Matters: Goal-setting as a team reinforces unity and encourages couples to work collaboratively toward a stronger relationship.

Scripture Reflection

Scripture: "But grow in the grace and knowledge of our Lord and Savior Jesus Christ. To him be glory both now and forever! Amen." (2 Peter 3:18)

Takeaways:

1. **Growth Is Continuous:** Personal and spiritual growth is a lifelong journey, essential for thriving in both individual and relational contexts.

2. **Grace Is Key:** Growing in grace means extending kindness and patience to yourself and your partner as you both work toward change.

3. **Knowledge Empowers:** Pursuing knowledge about yourself, your partner, and God's design for relationships equips you to navigate challenges with wisdom.

Goal for Chapter 7

Goal: Identify one personal goal and one shared goal to focus on this month. Create a plan for how you'll support each other in achieving these goals, and schedule a follow-up discussion to celebrate progress and adjust as needed.

Chapter 8

A Vision for Your World

Many couples struggle because they lack a clear vision for their world. When two worlds come together, the absence of a shared focus can cause confusion, misunderstandings, and unnecessary conflict. Without a vision, it's easy for worlds to collide rather than merge harmoniously.

In the previous chapter, we discussed setting personal goals to improve your own world. Now, it's time to build on that foundation and focus on a shared vision—one that brings clarity and purpose to your relationship. A vision acts as a guide, keeping both partners aligned and providing a framework for making decisions together.

Why Vision Matters

A vision for your world doesn't have to be overly complicated. It could simply mean committing to a life together forever. But even a simple vision like that requires planning and intentional actions to make it a reality.

Without a shared vision, couples often drift apart because there's no unified direction. Conflicts tend to escalate, misunderstandings become harder to resolve, and the relationship feels stagnant. But with a vision, there's a shared purpose that both partners can work toward, reducing friction and creating a sense of unity.

Our Story: Building a Vision Together

I'll never forget the day my wife and I sat down at Applebee's just after a month of being engaged. Over lunch, we grabbed a napkin and wrote down some of the things we wanted to accomplish together. That moment became the foundation for our shared vision, and it shaped the course of our relationship and our lives.

The name we gave to our plans was *Together Incorporated.* At the time, we didn't realize how significant that vision would be. We dreamed of buying real estate, starting businesses, and working together to build something meaningful. Those initial conversations and plans became the blueprint for everything we've accomplished since then.

Looking back over the past 27 years, I'm proud to say that we achieved everything we wrote down on that napkin and more. We bought several properties together, including a commercial property with 11 units, which now provides us with a solid financial foundation. We've started and managed multiple businesses, and we continue to work side by side, building and growing together.

The Power of Agreement

The key to our success wasn't just having a vision—it was our ability to agree on that vision and prioritize it. When both partners are on the same page about where they're headed, it becomes much easier to make decisions and navigate challenges.

For example, we've never had and major disagreements about how to raise our children. From the start, we agreed on our approach to parenting, and that unity has paid off. We believe it gave the four of them the foundation they needed to thrive with core principles instilled in them.

Of course, no relationship is without its challenges. But having a shared vision has helped us overcome those challenges. When conflicts arise, we remind ourselves of the vision we set for our relationship. That vision acts as an anchor, grounding us and giving us the perspective we need to move forward.

Creating a Vision for Your World

If you don't already have a shared vision for your relationship, it's never too late to create one. Start by sitting down with your partner and having an honest conversation about what you both want for your future.

Ask yourselves questions like:

- Where do we see ourselves in five, ten, or twenty years?

- What do we want to accomplish together?
- How can we support each other's individual goals while working toward a shared vision?

Write down your answers and use them as a guide for your relationship. Your vision doesn't have to be perfect or set in stone—it's something that can evolve over time. The important thing is that you have a direction to work toward together.

Staying Focused on the Vision

Life will inevitably bring challenges, and there will be times when conflicts or distractions threaten to derail your relationship. But when you have a vision, you have something to come back to.

Whenever my wife and I face a difficult moment, we remind ourselves of the vision we set all those years ago. We reflect on the purpose of our relationship and the goals we've achieved together. This practice has helped us stay aligned and strengthened our bond over time.

Reducing Conflict Through Unity

The more you and your partner can get on the same page about your vision, the less room there is for conflict to take hold. When you both know what you're working toward, it becomes easier to prioritize the relationship over individual differences.

Having a shared vision also creates a sense of accountability. When both partners are committed to the same goals, they're more likely to act in ways that support those goals rather than undermine them.

Moving Forward

A vision for your world is more than just a plan—it's a commitment to work together, grow together, and build a life that reflects your shared values and dreams. It provides direction, reduces conflict, and creates a sense of unity that strengthens your relationship.

Take the time to sit down with your partner and create a vision for your world. Write it down, refer to it often, and let it guide you through the ups and downs of life. With a clear vision and a commitment to work together, you can create a world that is not only strong but also full of purpose and joy.

Exercises for Chapter 8: A Vision for Your World

Exercise 1: Reflect and Share – "Envisioning Our Future"

Prompt: Take time separately to reflect on the following questions:

1. Where do you see our relationship in 5, 10, and 20 years?
2. What are three specific goals you want us to accomplish as a couple?
3. What values are most important for our relationship to uphold?

Once you've reflected, come together and share your answers, discussing similarities and differences in your visions.

Why This Exercise Matters: This activity helps both partners articulate their desires and align their visions for the relationship. By sharing openly, it fosters understanding and sets the stage for collaborative planning.

Exercise 2: Practical Action – "Creating Our Vision Statement"

Prompt: Together, write a vision statement for your relationship. Include:

- A shared purpose or mission for your relationship (e.g., "To grow in love, faith, and support for one another").
- Specific goals (e.g., building a strong financial foundation, nurturing a loving family, or creating a legacy).
- A commitment to how you will navigate challenges (e.g., "We will approach conflicts with patience and prioritize unity").

Display this statement somewhere visible in your home as a daily reminder of your shared vision.

Why This Exercise Matters: A written vision statement provides clarity and focus. It acts as a constant reminder of what you're working toward as a couple and helps guide decisions.

Exercise 3: Discussion – "Prioritizing Our Vision"

Prompt: Identify one area of your relationship that has been a source of tension or distraction from your shared goals. Discuss:

- How has this issue affected our vision?
- What changes can we make to address it and realign with our goals?
- How can we hold each other accountable while being supportive?

Why This Exercise Matters: This exercise encourages honest conversations about obstacles that may hinder progress. By addressing issues together, couples can strengthen their commitment to their vision.

Exercise 4: Goal-Setting – "Taking the First Step"

Prompt: Choose one specific goal from your vision and outline three actionable steps to start working toward it this month. For example:

- If your goal is financial stability, steps might include creating a joint budget, setting a savings goal, or attending a financial planning workshop.
- If your goal is emotional growth, steps might include scheduling weekly check-ins, reading a relationship book together, or attending couples counseling.

Commit to a timeline for completing these steps and celebrate your progress together.

Why This Exercise Matters: This exercise turns abstract goals into actionable steps, ensuring that your vision moves from concept to reality.

Scripture Reflection

Scripture: "Write the vision and make it plain on tablets, that hc may run who reads it." (IIabakkuk 2:2)

Takeaways:

1. **Clarity Leads to Action:** A clear, written vision provides direction and motivation.
2. **Shared Understanding:** When both partners understand and agree on the vision, they can move forward with unity and purpose.

3. **Focus on the Future:** A well-defined vision helps couples stay focused on long-term goals, even amidst challenges.

Goal for Chapter 8

Goal: Draft a shared vision for your relationship this week, including specific goals and values. Commit to revisiting it quarterly to track progress, refine your goals, and stay aligned as a couple.

Chapter 9

Conquering the World Together

Now that we've discussed the importance of having a vision as a couple, it's time to put that vision into action. Chapter 9, *Conquering the World Together*, focuses on collaboration, unity, and actionable steps to achieve shared dreams and goals.

One of the biggest challenges I've seen in couples I've counseled is that they often come together but live separate visions. This creates a tug-of-war dynamic where each person is pulling in opposite directions, leading to frustration and stagnation. Instead of working together as a unified team, they spin their wheels trying to accomplish individual goals while neglecting the power of their partnership.

The Power of Partnership

The Bible says in **Ecclesiastes 4:9**, *"Two are better than one, because they have a good return for their labor."* When two people work toward the same purpose, they can accomplish far more than they ever could alone. This is why unity in a relationship is so important. When you align your efforts, compromise where necessary, and support each other, you become an unstoppable force.

It's important to understand that when two worlds come together, there will be friction. But that friction is an opportunity for growth and healing. The areas where one partner is broken can be balanced and strengthened by the other, and together, you can address the deficiencies in both of your worlds.

Turning Dreams Into Goals

The foundation of conquering the world as a couple begins with having shared dreams. These dreams provide a sense of purpose and direction for your relationship. But a dream without action is just a wish. You must turn those dreams into specific, actionable goals that you can work toward together.

Here's how you can take actionable steps as a couple:

1. **Define Your Goals:** Sit down together and discuss what you both want to achieve. This could include financial stability, career milestones, parenting goals, or even personal growth objectives.

2. **Create a Plan:** Break your goals into smaller, manageable steps. Assign responsibilities to each partner and set realistic timelines.

3. **Encourage Each Other:** Support each other along the way. When one person feels discouraged, the other should step in with motivation and reassurance.

A Personal Example

When my wife and I first got together, we decided early on that we wanted to raise our children without outside influences that could potentially harm them. We agreed that she would adjust her career trajectory to ensure the kids had stability at home, while I would take on the financial responsibilities.

This wasn't an easy decision, but it worked because we were united in our vision. I never made her feel that the money I earned wasn't hers, and we shared everything equally. Over the course of our 27-year marriage, we've never had separate bank accounts or divided finances. This level of unity has been a cornerstone of our success as a couple.

The Importance of Collaboration

Collaboration is at the heart of conquering the world as a couple. It means sharing responsibilities, making joint decisions, and being accountable to each other. When one person struggles, the other steps in to help.

For example, if one partner is dealing with a personal challenge—whether it's emotional, financial, or career-related—it's not just their struggle; it's a challenge for both partners to address together. Adopting this mindset strengthens the relationship and ensures that no one feels isolated or unsupported.

Seeking Help When Needed

If conflicts or challenges arise that feel too difficult to handle on your own, seeking therapy or counseling can be incredibly beneficial. Individual therapy can help you address personal issues, while couples therapy can provide tools for improving communication and resolving conflicts. The goal is to ensure that nothing stands in the way of your shared vision and goals.

Celebrate Your Milestones

As you achieve goals together, it's important to celebrate those milestones. This doesn't mean extravagant celebrations; it could be something as simple as a weekend getaway or a special dinner. These moments of celebration reinforce the bond between you and remind you of what you've accomplished together.

For example, my wife and I have always made it a point to reward ourselves after achieving a major goal. Whether it was buying a new property, reaching a financial milestone, or raising our children successfully, we took the time to acknowledge our hard work and celebrate as a team.

Staying United Through Challenges

One of the biggest misconceptions about relationships is that love alone is enough to sustain them. The truth is, love needs to be paired with commitment, effort, and understanding. Even when my wife and I faced moments of frustration or disagreement, we never allowed those moments to derail our partnership.

For us, the key was always understanding that even during difficult times, we were on the same team. Bad days didn't mean we stopped loving each other or working toward our goals. Instead, we used those moments to grow closer and strengthen our bond.

Building an Extraordinary World Together

Conquering the world as a couple is about more than achieving external success—it's about building a life that reflects love, unity, and shared purpose. The world you create together is a reflection of the effort, dedication, and commitment you both bring to the relationship.

Your world is what you make of it. Whether it's raising children, pursuing careers, or simply building a life filled with love and joy, the possibilities are endless when you work together. As you continue this journey, remember that every challenge you face is an opportunity to grow stronger as a couple.

Make your world extraordinary. Together, there's nothing you can't conquer.

Exercises for Chapter 9: Conquering the World Together

Exercise 1: Shared Dreams – "Dream Big Together"

Prompt: Sit down with your partner and share your individual dreams. Then, discuss:

1. What are three dreams we have in common?
2. How can we combine our individual aspirations to create a shared dream?
3. Are there any dreams we've been neglecting as a couple that we want to pursue together?

Write down your shared dreams and keep them in a visible place to remind you of your shared purpose.

Why This Exercise Matters: This activity strengthens unity by aligning individual aspirations with shared goals. It encourages open communication about what each person values and desires for the future.

Exercise 2: Goal Breakdown – "From Dream to Action"

Prompt: Choose one of your shared dreams and break it into actionable steps:

- What is the ultimate goal?

- What are three smaller steps we can take toward achieving it?
- Who will take responsibility for each step, and what's the timeline?

Set regular check-ins to assess progress and adjust your plan as needed.

Why This Exercise Matters: This exercise focuses on turning dreams into practical goals, ensuring that the vision for your relationship becomes a reality through teamwork and accountability.

Exercise 3: Overcoming Obstacles – "When We Struggle"

Prompt: Reflect on challenges you've faced as a couple. Discuss:

1. What was a recent challenge that tested our partnership?
2. How did we handle it?
3. What could we do differently next time to overcome challenges more effectively?

Commit to one new strategy for addressing future struggles, such as improved communication or seeking outside support when needed.

Why This Exercise Matters: This exercise helps couples reflect on past conflicts and prepare for future challenges. It emphasizes growth and collaboration in overcoming obstacles together.

Exercise 4: Celebrate Success – "Milestone Rewards"

Prompt: Think about a goal or milestone you're currently working toward as a couple. Plan a reward for when you achieve it, such as:

- A special date night.
- A weekend getaway.
- A heartfelt exchange of letters acknowledging each other's contributions.

After celebrating, discuss how the milestone strengthened your relationship and what you learned from the process.

Why This Exercise Matters: Celebrating milestones reinforces the bond between partners and acknowledges the hard work they've put into their shared journey. It also creates positive memories that strengthen the relationship.

Scripture Reflection

Scripture: "Two are better than one, because they have a good return for their labor." (Ecclesiastes 4:9)

Takeaways:

1. **Partnership Enhances Productivity:** Working together allows couples to achieve more than they could individually.
2. **Unity Brings Strength:** A united effort creates resilience and fosters growth in the relationship.
3. **Shared Success is Rewarding:** Accomplishments feel more meaningful when celebrated as a team.

Goal for Chapter 9

Goal: Choose one shared dream this week and outline the steps needed to achieve it. Assign roles, set a timeline, and commit to celebrating your progress as a couple.

Chapter 10

A New World Order

As couples grow together, they naturally go through cycles of change. These cycles often involve navigating challenges, building new habits, and letting go of old patterns that no longer serve the relationship. This process of transformation is what I call *A New World Order*.

When two people commit to creating a life together, it's not just about blending their worlds; it's about establishing a new, shared world with its own norms, values, and practices. Just as believers in Christ are called to become new creations, relationships must also evolve, shedding old habits and embracing new ones that foster unity, growth, and mutual understanding.

Renewing Your Relationship

The Bible emphasizes the importance of renewal in Colossians 3:10: "And have put on the new self, which is being renewed in knowledge in the image of its Creator." This idea extends beyond personal transformation and into our relationships. Old patterns of behavior—whether they involve unhealthy communication, lingering conflicts, or ineffective habits—must be replaced with deliberate, constructive practices that nurture the partnership.

For instance, if past disagreements led to prolonged periods of silence, a New World Order requires a shift toward addressing and resolving conflicts sooner. As Ephesians 4:26 reminds us, "Do not let the sun go down while you are still angry." Allowing disputes to linger only creates emotional distance. Instead, aim to tackle issues before the day ends. While not every problem can be resolved immediately, making communication and reconciliation a consistent priority will strengthen your bond and pave the way for lasting harmony.

Establishing New Norms

A New World Order is about creating new norms that promote harmony and progress in your relationship. This involves identifying the habits and behaviors that no longer serve you and replacing them with practices that foster growth.

For instance:

- **Rebuilding After Chaos:** When conflict arises, prioritize rebuilding the relationship immediately. Don't let dysfunction linger. Address the issue, find common ground, and move forward.

- **Prioritizing What Matters:** Agree on the hierarchy of priorities in your relationship, such as spirituality, family goals, career aspirations, and finances. This prevents unnecessary arguments and ensures you're both working toward the same objectives.

- **Balancing Independence and Interdependence:** While it's important to maintain individuality, your relationship should always come first. Meet regularly to discuss individual needs and ensure they align with your shared goals.

Flexibility and Adaptability

Just like the world around us is constantly changing, relationships must also evolve to adapt to new circumstances. Flexibility is key to maintaining balance and preventing your shared world from breaking under pressure.

Revisiting your couple's goals periodically is an important part of this process. Life changes—careers shift, children grow, and external challenges arise. By staying flexible and open to adjustments, you can ensure that your relationship remains on course even as circumstances change.

For example, if one partner faces an unexpected career transition, the other partner may need to step in and adjust their role in the relationship temporarily. This kind of grace and adaptability is what sustains the New World Order in your relationship.

Grace in Execution

One of the most critical aspects of a New World Order is offering grace to one another. No one executes plans perfectly, and everyone has strengths and weaknesses. In my own marriage of over 27 years, there were many times when my wife and I had to go around the block a few times—meaning we had to revisit the same issues until we could align and move forward.

While my wife was always on board with our visions and plans, sometimes the way she executed them differed from how I would have. Instead of getting frustrated, I learned to offer grace and support. Similarly, there were areas where I fell short, and she had to pick up the slack. This mutual understanding and willingness to cover for each other is what allowed us to keep moving forward.

Letting Go of What No Longer Serves

One of the greatest barriers to progress in a relationship is holding onto habits or patterns that no longer serve you. It's amazing how long people continue behaviors that aren't working, wasting precious time that could be spent building something better.

In the New World Order, couples must actively identify and let go of these outdated practices. For example:

- If unresolved conflicts lead to repeated arguments, commit to better communication.
- If poor financial habits are holding you back, agree on a budget and stick to it.
- If you've been prioritizing individual pursuits over shared goals, realign your focus.

The time you spend clinging to unproductive behaviors is time you'll never get back. Instead, use that time to build new, healthier habits that bring you closer to your shared vision.

Personal Illustration

In my own experience, there were times when my wife and I had to pause and reassess our priorities to move forward. We knew what we wanted to achieve, but sometimes execution became an issue. There were things she excelled at that I struggled with and vice versa. Offering grace to one another in these moments was essential.

For example, I've always been driven and goal-oriented, while my wife approaches things with a more measured pace. Early on, this created frustration for me, but I learned to appreciate her way of doing things and to adjust my expectations. In turn, she showed me grace in areas where I needed time to grow or refine my approach.

This mutual grace allowed us to stay aligned, even when life's challenges tried to pull us apart.

Building Your New World Order

A New World Order isn't just a concept—it's a commitment to growth, collaboration, and adaptability in your relationship. It's about shedding old habits and embracing new practices that reflect the vision you've set as a couple.

As you move forward, remember these key principles:

1. **Rebuild After Chaos:** Don't let conflicts linger; address them quickly and move forward.

2. **Set Clear Priorities:** Agree on what matters most in your relationship and stick to those priorities.

3. **Offer Grace:** Recognize that no one is perfect, and be willing to support each other through mistakes and setbacks.

4. **Stay Flexible:** Revisit your goals regularly and adjust as needed to stay on course.

By embracing these principles, you can create a relationship that thrives on unity, understanding, and shared purpose. Together, you can establish a New World Order that reflects the love, grace, and commitment you've built as a couple.

Exercises for Chapter 10: A New World Order

Exercise 1: Identify Old Patterns – "What Should We Let Go?"

Prompt: Individually write down three habits, behaviors, or practices in your relationship that no longer serve your partnership (e.g., unresolved arguments, poor financial habits, ignoring each other's emotional needs). Share your lists with each other and discuss:

- Why these patterns are unhelpful.
- How you can replace them with healthier practices.
- Commit to one action step to begin letting go of each habit.

Why This Exercise Matters: Identifying and letting go of unproductive habits clears space for growth and harmony. It also encourages open communication and mutual accountability.

Exercise 2: Set New Norms – "Our Relationship Blueprint"

Prompt: Together, create a "New World Order Blueprint" for your relationship. Discuss:

1. What new practices or habits would strengthen our relationship?
2. How will we rebuild quickly after disagreements?

3. What are three priorities we will focus on in the next six months?

Write these down and display them somewhere visible as a reminder of your commitment to building a stronger relationship.

Why This Exercise Matters: This activity ensures both partners are aligned and intentional about their shared goals, reducing confusion and creating unity.

Exercise 3: Grace Check-In – "How Can I Support You?"

Prompt: Schedule a weekly or biweekly "Grace Check-In" where you ask each other:

- What's something I can do to support you better this week?
- Are there areas where I've fallen short that we should address?
- What's one thing we can celebrate together this week?

Use this time to practice offering grace and understanding while also celebrating small wins.

Why This Exercise Matters: Regular check-ins foster connection, mutual support, and accountability. They create a safe space to address issues and celebrate progress.

Exercise 4: Flexibility in Action – "Adapting Together"

Prompt: Choose a current goal or challenge you're working on as a couple. Discuss:

1. What's working well?
2. What isn't working, and why?

3. How can we adjust our approach to achieve better results?

Agree on one adjustment to try for the next week and evaluate its effectiveness at your next Grace Check-In.

Why This Exercise Matters: Flexibility ensures your relationship stays adaptable to life's changes and challenges. It also encourages creative problem-solving and teamwork.

Scripture Reflection

Scripture: "See, I am doing a new thing! Now it springs up; do you not perceive it? I am making a way in the wilderness and streams in the wasteland." (Isaiah 43:19)

Takeaways:

1. **Embrace Renewal:** God is always working to bring new opportunities for growth and healing, even in the midst of challenges.
2. **See the Bigger Picture:** Recognizing God's work in your relationship requires attentiveness and faith.
3. **Hope in Transformation:** No matter how broken or dry the past may feel, God provides a path for restoration and flourishing.

Goal for Chapter 10

Goal: Choose one area in your relationship that needs renewal and commit to implementing a new practice or habit this week. Evaluate your progress during your next Grace Check-In.

Chapter 11

A World of Trouble

As couples navigate the complexities of their relationships, there will inevitably be moments when their worlds are tested in ways they never expected. This chapter, "A World of Trouble," dives into the reality that sometimes the challenges we face don't just come from external pressures—they stem from habits, patterns, or brokenness we've carried with us for years.

Trouble in a relationship doesn't always start with an argument or a misunderstanding. Sometimes, it's rooted in a personal struggle that spills over into the partnership. And when these moments arise, it's not uncommon for the relationship to feel like it's on shaky ground. However, as you'll see in this chapter, there's a path forward—even in the midst of chaos.

Personal Struggles, Shared Impact

In 2014, I found myself in the grip of an addiction I never saw coming. It started innocently enough: I was in Philadelphia for a recertification meeting and had an hour to kill before it began. Across the street from the 7-Eleven where I was grabbing snacks was a casino. With nothing else to do, I decided to spend $100 and see what would happen. To my surprise, I walked out an hour later with nearly $2,000.

The thrill of that moment was unlike anything I'd experienced in years. I thought to myself, *This is amazing—what if I can do this again?* After my meeting, I drove home, still thinking about the win. The next day, I found a casino closer to home, walked in with the same $100, and once again walked out with nearly $2,000. It seemed too good to be true—and, of course, it was.

Over the course of the next four years, I found myself trapped in the grip of a gambling addiction. What started as a harmless way to pass time quickly became an obsession. I was no longer chasing the thrill of winning; I was chasing the money I had already lost. I'd built my businesses in a way that gave me financial freedom, but instead of using that freedom wisely, I used it to spend hours in casinos, hoping for a comeback.

The Impact on My Relationship

At first, I didn't tell my wife what I was doing. I thought I could handle it on my own, and I didn't want to worry her. But after about a month, my habit started to catch up with me. My wife noticed that

$4,000 had gone missing from our bank account—twice. When she confronted me, I had no choice but to come clean.

She was disappointed, as anyone would be, but she didn't judge me. Instead, she warned me of the dangers of what I was doing. She told me she didn't think it was something I should continue, and she prayed for me. Despite her warnings, I couldn't stop. I was caught in a cycle of addiction that I couldn't seem to break.

Looking back, I see how my wife's approach made all the difference. While she didn't condone my behavior, she didn't shame me for it either. She joked with me at times—saying things like, "When are you going to learn?"—but she always supported me. When I finally admitted that I had a problem, she stood by me as I worked to overcome it.

The Role of Early Influences

As I reflected on how I got caught up in gambling, I realized that the seeds of this struggle had been planted long before 2014. When I was a child, my father taught me how to play cards. He was preparing to take my mother to Atlantic City and wanted to learn a specific game, so he practiced with me. I absorbed everything he taught me and eventually took a deck of cards to school, where I started winning money from classmates.

Later, I learned how to play dice games like CeeLo, and I became the "bank" in school games, beating kids out of their money. These experiences introduced me to the thrill of gambling at a young age. I didn't realize it at the time, but they were shaping how I would handle temptation and risk later in life.

When I walked into that casino in Philadelphia, it wasn't my first exposure to gambling. It was the culmination of years of familiarity with the world of gambling—a world that the enemy used to lure me into a destructive cycle.

The Enemy's Tactics

As I've shared in previous chapters, the enemy uses three primary tools to draw us away from God's plan: the lust of the flesh, the lust of the eyes, and the pride of life. For me, gambling represented all three. It fed my pride by making me believe I could outsmart the system. It satisfied the lust of my eyes by offering the allure of quick money. And it provided a temporary escape from the emotional pain I was feeling after the loss of my father.

The devil knows how to exploit our weaknesses, and he used my grief and curiosity to pull me deeper into a world of trouble. But what he didn't count on was the power of prayer and the support of a loving spouse.

Grace and Redemption

After four years of struggling with gambling, I finally broke free. It wasn't an easy process, and there were moments when I thought I would never escape. But through God's grace, my wife's prayers, and a commitment to honesty, I was able to leave that addiction behind.

Today, I'm back on track, focused on the original goals my wife and I set for our life together. I've even written a book about my experience, *Stop Gambling With Your Future: How to Stop Gambling Addiction Through Faith and Spiritual Warfare,* in the hope that my story will help others who are facing similar struggles.

Lessons Learned

This chapter isn't just about gambling—it's about the challenges that come when one partner falls into a world of trouble. Whether it's addiction, infidelity, or another form of brokenness, these moments can test a relationship in profound ways. But they can also serve as opportunities for growth, healing, and deeper connection.

Here are some key takeaways from my experience:

1. **Honesty is Crucial:** The first step to overcoming any struggle is admitting there's a problem. Hiding your struggles from your partner only creates more distance.

2. **Support Makes a Difference:** My wife's unwavering support and prayers were instrumental in my recovery. Even when she didn't understand my actions, she chose to stand by me.

3. **God's Grace is Sufficient:** No matter how far you've fallen, God's grace can redeem you. He can use even your darkest moments to bring about healing and transformation.

Moving Forward

If you or your partner find yourselves in a world of trouble, know that it's not the end. With honesty, support, and faith, you can overcome even the most difficult challenges. Remember, your relationship is a partnership. When one person struggles, it's an opportunity for both partners to come together and strengthen their bond.

A world of trouble doesn't have to define your relationship. It can be the catalyst for growth, healing, and a deeper connection with one another. Let this chapter serve as a reminder that even in the midst of chaos, there is hope.

Exercises for Chapter 11: A World of Trouble

Exercise 1: Recognizing a World of Trouble – "What Has Challenged Us?"

Prompt: Individually reflect on and write down three significant challenges or struggles that your relationship has faced. These could include financial strain, trust issues, or personal battles that affected the partnership. Share your lists with each other and discuss:

- How did these challenges impact our relationship?
- What did we learn from these experiences?
- How can we support each other better in similar situations moving forward?

Why This Exercise Matters: Acknowledging past challenges helps couples identify growth opportunities and creates a foundation for understanding and resilience when facing future difficulties.

Exercise 2: Identifying Triggers – "Where Does the Trouble Begin?"

Prompt: Each partner should individually list three personal triggers that have caused tension or conflict in the relationship.

Examples include stress, unresolved grief, or financial pressures. Then, together:

- Discuss how these triggers manifest in your behavior or responses.
- Identify one healthier coping mechanism for each trigger.
- Commit to supporting each other in recognizing and managing these triggers.

Why This Exercise Matters: Understanding triggers allows couples to address issues proactively and respond with empathy rather than judgment.

Exercise 3: Rebuilding After Trouble – "The Grace Formula"

Prompt: Discuss a recent conflict or challenging moment in your relationship. Together, explore the following:

1. What went wrong, and what emotions were involved?
2. What could we have done differently?
3. What steps can we take to rebuild trust or connection in the future?
4. How can we practice grace toward each other during difficult times?

Why This Exercise Matters: This activity emphasizes the importance of grace and constructive communication in rebuilding and strengthening the relationship after conflict.

Exercise 4: Support Through Troubles – "How Can I Be There for You?"

Prompt: Schedule a time to sit down together and ask each other these questions:

1. What is one challenge you're currently facing that you haven't fully shared with me?
2. How can I better support you in this area?
3. What's one thing I can do this week to make your world feel less heavy?

Write down each other's responses and commit to small, intentional actions to support one another.

Why This Exercise Matters: This exercise fosters vulnerability, empathy, and mutual support by encouraging open dialogue about unspoken struggles.

Scripture Reflection

Scripture: "Carry each other's burdens, and in this way you will fulfill the law of Christ." (Galatians 6:2)

Takeaways:

1. **Shared Burdens:** A strong relationship requires a willingness to support one another through life's difficulties.
2. **Christlike Love:** Demonstrating care and compassion fulfills God's purpose for our relationships.
3. **Healing Together:** Helping your partner navigate their challenges fosters unity and trust in the relationship.

Goal for Chapter 11

Goal: Identify one area of "trouble" in your relationship that needs immediate attention. Together, outline one step to address this issue and commit to following through this week.

Chapter 12

A World of Temptation

Temptation is everywhere. It doesn't knock loudly or announce itself—it sneaks in quietly, using the cracks in our emotional, spiritual, or relational foundations to create division. For couples, this world of temptation can be one of the greatest challenges they face together. It tests their commitment, patience, and ability to stand united.

In this chapter, I want to talk about the various forms of temptation, how they infiltrate relationships, and what you can do to guard against them. My own experiences—and the lessons I've learned—will serve as a foundation for helping you navigate the inevitable struggles that come with living in a world designed to distract and derail.

The Enemy's Strategy

The Bible gives us insight into the enemy's agenda in John 10:10: "The thief comes only to steal and kill and destroy; I have come that they may have life, and have it to the full." This verse clearly outlines the contrasting goals of God and the devil. God desires for us to have an abundant life, one filled with love, joy, and purpose. The enemy, on the other hand, seeks to destroy everything God has built, including relationships.

One of the primary ways the enemy attacks is through temptation. He doesn't just focus on individuals; he targets couples, knowing that the strength of a marriage reflects God's covenant. We saw this tactic in the Garden of Eden, where the enemy's goal was to destroy humanity by targeting the first couple, Adam and Eve. The strategy hasn't changed—it's just evolved with the times.

In today's world, temptation comes in many forms: lust, pride, greed, emotional detachment, and distractions. If left unchecked, these forces can erode the foundation of a relationship, leaving both partners vulnerable to separation and division.

Personal Vulnerabilities

I know firsthand how temptation can creep in and create chaos. As I shared already with you my experience with gambling addiction and how it began while waiting for a meeting in Philadelphia. What started as harmless curiosity quickly spiraled into a full-blown addiction that consumed my time, money, and energy for four years.

But gambling wasn't the only temptation I've faced. Sexual temptation, emotional distance, and pride have all been challenges in my relationship. Temptation doesn't discriminate—it preys on our brokenness, using whatever it can to pull us further from God's plan for our lives and our relationships.

The Subtle Nature of Temptation

Not all temptations are as obvious as gambling or infidelity. Some are subtle, sneaking into our lives disguised as harmless habits or innocent interactions. Here are a few examples of how temptation can manifest in a relationship:

- **Social Media and Comparisons:** In the age of social media, we're constantly bombarded with images and stories that can make us question our own relationships. Seeing other couples' seemingly perfect lives can create dissatisfaction, leading to unnecessary conflict or resentment.

- **Emotional Infidelity:** This often starts innocently, such as confiding in a coworker or friend about your struggles. Over time, these interactions can develop into deeper emotional connections that undermine your marriage.

- **Neglect and Disconnection:** Spending excessive time on hobbies, work, or personal interests can leave your partner feeling isolated or undervalued. This creates a space for temptation to thrive, as one or both partners seek connection elsewhere.

- **Unaddressed Hurt:** When conflicts are left unresolved, they fester. Over time, this can lead to bitterness and a desire to seek solace outside the relationship.

Guarding Against Temptation

So, how do couples protect their relationship in a world filled with temptation? The answer lies in intentionality and unity. Here are some practical steps to consider:

1. **Open Communication:** Transparency is key. If you or your partner are feeling tempted—whether by a person, a habit, or a situation—it's crucial to talk about it. Secrets and lies only create distance.

2. **Boundaries:** Set clear boundaries to protect your relationship. This might include avoiding private time with members of the opposite sex, limiting social media use, or agreeing to share passwords for accountability.

3. **Accountability:** Be accountable to each other. Regularly check in to discuss how you're doing emotionally, spiritually, and relationally. This keeps both partners aligned and aware of each other's needs.

4. **Spiritual Practices:** Prayer and scripture are powerful tools for guarding against temptation. By inviting God into your relationship, you strengthen your bond and gain clarity in moments of doubt or struggle.

Understanding Paul's Guidance

One of the most impactful scriptures for couples dealing with sexual temptation is 1 Corinthians 7:5, where Paul advises: "Do not deprive each other except perhaps by mutual consent and for a time, so that you may devote yourselves to prayer. Then come together again so that Satan will not *tempt* you because of your **lack of self-control.**"

Let's break this down:

1. **Physical and Emotional Intimacy:** Paul emphasizes the importance of maintaining intimacy in a marriage. When couples neglect this aspect of their relationship, they create space for temptation to enter.

2. **Mutual Consent:** Decisions about separation—whether physical, emotional, or spiritual—should be made together, ensuring that neither partner feels abandoned or neglected.

3. **Reunification:** After a period of separation, it's essential to come back together and reaffirm your commitment. This strengthens the relationship and guards against external threats.

Lessons from My Journey

Reflecting on my own experiences with temptation, I've learned several key lessons that have helped me navigate this world and protect my marriage:

1. **Temptation is Inevitable:** It's not a matter of if but when. Recognizing this reality allows you to prepare and guard your relationship proactively.
2. **Grace is Essential:** Neither you nor your partner will navigate temptation perfectly. Offer each other grace and forgiveness as you work through challenges together.
3. **God's Strength is Sufficient:** On our own, we are weak. But with God's strength, we can resist even the most persistent temptations. Lean on Him for guidance and support.

Moving Forward

This world is full of temptation, but it doesn't have to define your relationship. By staying vigilant, communicating openly, and grounding yourselves in God's Word, you can navigate even the most challenging moments with confidence and unity.

Temptation is a test, but it's also an opportunity—to strengthen your bond, grow closer to God, and build a relationship that reflects His love and grace. Remember, the enemy's goal is to steal, kill, and destroy, but God's plan is for you to have life—and have it abundantly.

Exercises for Chapter 12: A World of Temptation

Exercise 1: Identify Personal Temptations

Prompt: Individually reflect on the areas in your life where you feel most tempted or vulnerable. Write down:

- What specific temptations challenge you most (e.g., distractions, unfaithful thoughts, excessive social media use)?
- How these temptations could affect your relationship if left unchecked.
- Steps you can take to address or avoid these temptations.

Share your list with your partner, focusing on ways you can support each other in resisting these challenges.

Why This Exercise Matters: Openly identifying and discussing personal temptations fosters trust and accountability. It also allows couples to create a united front against external threats to their relationship.

Exercise 2: Set Boundaries Together

Prompt: As a couple, discuss areas where you feel boundaries might be needed to guard your relationship from temptation. This could include:

- Social media habits (e.g., limiting time spent online or avoiding interactions that could spark jealousy).

- Time spent with friends or coworkers of the opposite sex.

- Protecting your relationship from outside influences, like workaholism or substance use.

Agree on at least three boundaries to implement and revisit them after one month to evaluate their effectiveness.

Why This Exercise Matters: Setting boundaries as a team creates a shared commitment to protecting the relationship. It also establishes clear expectations, reducing the likelihood of misunderstandings or conflicts.

Exercise 3: Build an "Armor of Affirmation"

Prompt: Write a list of affirmations to share with your partner, focusing on their value, attractiveness, and importance in your life. Examples include:

- "I appreciate everything you do for our family."
- "You are the most beautiful person in my life."
- "I feel secure and loved when I'm with you."

Exchange your lists and make a commitment to speak one affirmation to each other daily for the next month.

Why This Exercise Matters: Regular affirmations strengthen emotional intimacy and reduce the likelihood of seeking validation elsewhere. They create a positive atmosphere that reinforces love and connection.

Exercise 4: Create a "Temptation-Free Zone"

Prompt: Dedicate specific times or spaces in your relationship as temptation-free zones. For example:

- Have "no-phone" dinners where both partners disconnect from devices.
- Set aside one evening a week for intentional connection (e.g., a date night, prayer time, or deep conversation).
- Identify activities or habits that create distance and commit to replacing them with bonding activities.

Check in weekly to assess how these zones are helping strengthen your relationship.

Why This Exercise Matters: A temptation-free zone provides a safe space for couples to reconnect and prioritize each other over distractions. It encourages healthy habits that build trust and intimacy.

Scripture Reflection

Scripture: "No temptation has overtaken you except what is common to mankind. And God is faithful; he will not let you be tempted beyond what you can bear. But when you are tempted, he will also provide a way out so that you can endure it." (1 Corinthians 10:13)

Takeaways:

1. **Temptation is Universal:** Everyone faces temptation, but acknowledging it is the first step toward overcoming it.

2. **Rely on God's Faithfulness:** Trust that God will provide the strength and guidance needed to resist and overcome temptation.

3. **Find the Escape Route:** Be vigilant in identifying ways to avoid or escape situations that could harm your relationship.

Goal for Chapter 12

Goal: Identify one specific temptation that poses a challenge in your relationship. Commit to implementing a strategy to avoid or overcome it, and evaluate your progress together after two weeks.

Chapter 13

You Rock My World

In the ups and downs of life, relationships are meant to be a safe haven—a world where you and your partner create joy, passion, and connection. This chapter, "You Rock My World," is about rediscovering and maintaining that spark. It's about making intentional choices to nurture your relationship so that both partners feel loved, valued, and deeply connected.

While the title may evoke memories of Michael Jackson's iconic song, the sentiment behind it holds true: your goal in a relationship should be to "rock" your partner's world. You should strive to consistently meet their emotional, mental, and physical needs in ways that strengthen your bond and make your world together extraordinary.

Breaking Through Comfort Zones

As relationships grow over time, it's easy to fall into patterns of comfort. The little things you once did to woo your partner may slowly fade, replaced by routine and familiarity. While longevity in a relationship is a blessing, it shouldn't lead to complacency. The same energy and creativity you brought in the beginning should be maintained throughout your partnership.

I've personally learned the importance of breaking through comfort zones. For instance, I make it a point to be spontaneous with my wife. Whether it's sending a thoughtful text during the day, surprising her with her favorite dessert, or planning an unexpected date night, I've found that small gestures go a long way in keeping the relationship vibrant. Just yesterday, I sent her a text thanking her for being an amazing mother to our children. It wasn't a special occasion—it was simply something I felt and wanted to express.

These small moments of appreciation remind your partner that they are seen, valued, and loved.

Understanding Your Partner's Needs

Rocking your partner's world begins with understanding their needs—both spoken and unspoken. It's about being intentional in learning what makes them feel loved and appreciated. From my perspective as a man, I've discovered that understanding my wife's desires—both emotional and physical—is crucial.

For example, early in our marriage, I had to address issues with premature ejaculation a few times. I would be so turned on by my wife that I would let things happen early, LOL!. I took the time to educate myself on techniques that would allow me to better satisfy her way longer. This wasn't just about improving physical intimacy; it was about showing her that I cared enough to adjust and prioritize her needs even when she didn't ask me to. The result was being able to last long enough to give multiple orgasms and ejaculate at will.

Similarly, women can rock their partner's world by understanding what stimulates and motivates him. Men are often visually stimulated, and while this may seem like a small detail, it's a significant one. A woman who takes the time to visually appeal to her partner—whether through her choice of clothing, her confidence, or her playfulness—can create a deeper connection. Just as men should prioritize their wife's needs, women should also invest effort into understanding and meeting their husband's.

The Role of Intentional Effort

Rocking your partner's world requires intentional effort. It's about creating a relationship that thrives on mutual care, respect, and creativity. Here are a few ways to maintain that spark:

1. **Spontaneity:** Don't let routine dull the excitement in your relationship. Plan surprises, take time to celebrate small wins, and inject creativity into your interactions.

2. **Compliments and Affirmations:** Regularly tell your partner what you appreciate about them. Whether it's their sense of humor, their cooking, or their dedication to the family, let them know they're valued.

3. **Physical Intimacy:** Physical connection is a vital part of any relationship. Take the time to understand your partner's preferences and desires, and work to meet them in ways that bring fulfillment to both of you.

4. **Quality Time:** In a world full of distractions, dedicating uninterrupted time to your partner can make all the difference. Put down your phone, turn off the TV, and focus on each other.

Building a Shared World

When you commit to rocking your partner's world, you're not just investing in them—you're investing in the shared world you're building together. This world should be a sanctuary where both partners feel loved, secure, and fulfilled. It's a place where you work together to shield each other from the challenges of the outside world and create a space filled with joy and connection.

Biblical Foundations for Intimacy

The Bible offers wisdom on how couples can strengthen their bond and foster intimacy. The Song of Solomon, in particular, is a beautiful example of God's design for love and passion in a marriage. Here are four scriptures from the Song of Solomon that highlight the importance of intimacy:

1. **Song of Solomon 2:16:** "My beloved is mine, and I am his; he browses among the lilies."

   - This verse emphasizes the mutual belonging and joy that comes from a deep, intimate connection.

2. **Song of Solomon 4:7:** "You are altogether beautiful, my love; there is no flaw in you."

   - This verse reminds us of the power of affirming and celebrating your partner's beauty—both inside and out.

3. **Song of Solomon 1:2:** "Let him kiss me with the kisses of his mouth—for your love is more delightful than wine."

   - This verse highlights the passion and delight that should be present in a loving relationship.

4. **Song of Solomon 8:6:** "Place me like a seal over your heart, like a seal on your arm; for love is as strong as death, its jealousy unyielding as the grave."

   - This verse underscores the unbreakable bond and commitment that love brings.

Moving Beyond Physical Connection

While physical intimacy is essential, rocking your partner's world also involves emotional and spiritual connection. The Bible teaches us that love is patient, kind, and selfless (1 Corinthians 13:4-7). These qualities should be evident in how you treat your partner, how you handle conflicts, and how you support each other through life's challenges.

For example, I often remind myself to speak life into my wife. Instead of criticizing or complaining, I focus on lifting her up and encouraging her. By doing so, I create an environment where she feels safe and valued—a place where her world is rocked in the best possible way.

131

A Call to Action

As you reflect on this chapter, ask yourself: What can I do today to rock my partner's world? Whether it's a simple gesture of appreciation, an act of service, or a renewed effort to connect on a deeper level, take the initiative to show your partner that they are your priority.

When you commit to rocking your partner's world, you're not just enhancing your relationship—you're creating a legacy of love, passion, and connection that will inspire others. Let your actions speak louder than words, and let your love be a testament to the power of intentional effort.

Exercises for Chapter 13: You Rock My World

Exercise 1: Rediscover Each Other

Prompt: Schedule a time to sit down together and reflect on your relationship. Individually answer the following questions, then share your responses with each other:

- What was one thing I did early in our relationship that made you feel loved or appreciated?
- What is something I do now that you enjoy?
- What is one new thing I could start doing to show you how much I value you?

Why This Exercise Matters: This exercise helps couples reconnect by rediscovering what initially drew them together. It also opens the door for intentional actions that can reignite the passion and connection in the relationship.

Exercise 2: Surprise Your Partner

Prompt: Over the next week, plan a small surprise for your partner based on their preferences. It could be a handwritten note, their favorite meal, or a planned date night. After the surprise, take a few minutes to discuss how it made them feel and how you can incorporate surprises into your relationship more often.

Why This Exercise Matters: Thoughtful surprises show your partner that you're paying attention to their needs and desires. They create excitement and foster a sense of being cherished and valued.

Exercise 3: Create a "World Rocking" Checklist

Prompt: Work together to create a list of five things that would "rock your world" as a couple. This could include:

- Small daily gestures (e.g., morning kisses or thank-you notes).
- Weekly habits (e.g., intentional conversations or a date night).
- Long-term goals (e.g., planning a vacation or achieving a shared milestone).

Post this checklist somewhere visible and check in monthly to ensure you're both staying on track.

Why This Exercise Matters: A shared checklist promotes teamwork and accountability, helping both partners stay intentional about nurturing the relationship.

Exercise 4: Focus on Physical and Emotional Intimacy

Prompt: Schedule an uninterrupted evening to focus on physical and emotional intimacy. Start by having a heartfelt conversation about:

- What physical gestures make you feel most loved.
- What emotional connections deepen your bond.

- Any areas where you feel improvement is needed.

From there, plan an evening that incorporates these elements (e.g., a candlelit dinner, a walk under the stars, or simply spending quality time together without distractions).

Why This Exercise Matters: Physical and emotional intimacy are equally important in maintaining a healthy relationship. This exercise encourages vulnerability and deepens the connection between partners.

Scripture Reflection

Scripture: "You are altogether beautiful, my love; there is no flaw in you." (Song of Solomon 4:7)

Takeaways:

1. **Celebrate Your Partner:** Acknowledge and affirm your partner's beauty, value, and uniqueness.
2. **Focus on Positivity:** Instead of dwelling on flaws or shortcomings, focus on the attributes that make your partner special.
3. **Build Each Other Up:** Use your words and actions to uplift your partner, creating a foundation of mutual respect and admiration.

Goal for Chapter 13

Goal: Commit to one consistent action that will "rock your partner's world." Whether it's daily affirmations, more physical affection, or planning regular surprises, make it a priority and check in after two weeks to discuss its impact.

Chapter 14

What in the World Happened?

As relationships grow and evolve, it's natural for unexpected changes to arise. Over time, you and your partner may find yourselves facing moments where one of you seems different, introduces new habits, or develops unexpected perspectives. These shifts can leave you wondering, *What in the world happened?*

This chapter dives into these moments of surprise and evolution, exploring how to navigate the shifts in a way that strengthens your bond rather than creating distance.

Change is Inevitable

One of the constants in life is change. As individuals, we are constantly evolving. Experiences, interactions, and even small moments of reflection shape who we are, often leading to shifts in our thoughts, behaviors, and habits.

For couples, this evolution can be both exciting and challenging. While growth is vital for any relationship, it can sometimes introduce unexpected friction. You may find yourself questioning your partner's choices, wondering about their new priorities, or trying to understand where a sudden change originated.

For example, early in my relationship, I introduced a new position during an intimate moment that raised an eyebrow from my wife. Her immediate response was, "Where in the world did that come from?" She was genuinely curious, and honestly, it was something I'd seen elsewhere that I decided to try. Moments like these—when a new behavior appears without warning—can lead to confusion or even conflict if not addressed with honesty and openness.

Recognizing the Source of Change

Changes in behavior or habits don't appear out of thin air. Often, they are influenced by:

- **Social Circles:** People we interact with can introduce us to new ideas, habits, or beliefs. For example, your partner may suddenly use a slang word they picked up from friends or develop an interest in a new hobby.

- **Technology:** Social media and apps can become significant distractions. I remember when my kids introduced my wife to TikTok, and suddenly, she was spending hours scrolling through videos. At first, I was surprised, wondering where this newfound habit came from, but I quickly realized it was just a phase.

138

- **Family Influence:** Sometimes, past experiences or childhood lessons resurface later in life. For instance, when our first child started walking, my wife and I had a heated discussion about discipline. She introduced a stricter approach that I hadn't seen before, and I had to ask, "Where did that come from?" It turned out it was a method her mother used.

Understanding the source of change can help you approach these moments with empathy rather than judgment.

Balancing Embracing Change and Maintaining Stability

While it's important to remain open to your partner's evolution, it's equally crucial to ensure these changes don't disrupt the stability of your relationship. Here are some strategies to strike that balance:

1. **Keep an Open Mind:** Even if a new habit or behavior feels foreign to you, avoid dismissing it outright. Take the time to understand why your partner has embraced it and whether it aligns with your shared values.

2. **Communicate Calmly:** When something new arises, express your feelings without judgment. For instance, if your partner suddenly decides to explore veganism and stops cooking meat, discuss how this change can work for both of you.

3. **Establish Boundaries Together:** Not all changes are beneficial. If a new habit starts to affect your relationship negatively—like excessive time spent on social media—work together to set boundaries.

4. **Celebrate Growth:** Some changes can be incredibly positive, bringing new energy and excitement into your relationship. Acknowledge and encourage the ways your partner is growing and evolving.

When Change Causes Conflict

Sometimes, new behaviors or priorities can create tension. You may feel blindsided or even betrayed if your partner shifts in a way that seems to go against the foundation of your relationship.

For example, imagine you've built your relationship on mutual trust and openness, but suddenly your partner starts keeping secrets or withholding information. In these moments, it's important to:

- **Stay Curious, Not Confrontational:** Instead of accusing your partner, ask open-ended questions like, "I've noticed this change—can you tell me more about it?"
- **Revisit Your Shared Vision:** Remind yourselves of the goals and values you've set as a couple. Use these as a guide to determine whether the new habit aligns with your relationship's direction.
- **Seek Compromise:** Not every change needs to be fully embraced or fully rejected. Find a middle ground that respects both partners' needs and preferences.

Embracing Your Partner's Growth

While some changes may feel unsettling, others can be opportunities for growth and connection. For instance, if your partner takes up a new hobby or interest, consider joining them or showing genuine interest. These shared experiences can deepen your bond and create new memories together.

I've learned that the best way to navigate change is to approach it with grace and curiosity. Rather than seeing your partner's evolution as a threat, view it as an opportunity to grow closer. Ask questions, express support, and find ways to adapt together.

Finding Common Ground

At the heart of every relationship is the need for connection and understanding. When unexpected changes arise, focus on maintaining that connection by:

- **Expressing Vulnerability:** Share your feelings honestly, whether you're excited, confused, or concerned about the change.
- **Listening Actively:** Take the time to truly hear your partner's perspective without interrupting or assuming.
- **Staying Flexible:** Be willing to adjust your own expectations and routines to accommodate your partner's growth.

Moving Forward Together

Every relationship will encounter moments where one partner's evolution leaves the other wondering, *What in the world happened?* These moments are not roadblocks—they're opportunities to deepen your understanding of each other and strengthen your bond.

By staying open, communicating effectively, and working together to navigate change, you can turn these surprises into stepping stones toward a stronger, more resilient partnership. Remember, growth is a natural part of life—and when embraced with love and respect, it can bring you closer than ever.

Exercises for Chapter 14: What in the World Happened?

Exercise 1: Identifying the Source of Change – "Where Did That Come From?"

Prompt: Individually, think of a recent behavior, habit, or change in your partner that surprised you. Write it down and ask yourself:

1. How did this new habit or behavior make you feel?
2. What do you think might have influenced this change (e.g., friends, family, social media)?
3. Is this change positive, neutral, or negative for your relationship?

After reflecting, share your thoughts with your partner and listen to their perspective about the change.

Why This Exercise Matters: This exercise fosters understanding by encouraging curiosity instead of judgment. It helps you approach changes with empathy and open communication, rather than reacting defensively.

Exercise 2: Healthy Exploration – "What New Things Can We Embrace Together?"

Prompt: As a couple, list three new habits, interests, or experiences you'd like to explore together. Discuss:

1. Why do these interest you?

143

2. How can we integrate these new activities into our relationship?

3. What benefits do you think these changes could bring to our partnership?

Make a plan to try one of the new activities within the next month.

Why This Exercise Matters: By exploring new things together, you create opportunities for growth and connection. This exercise shifts the focus from individual changes to shared experiences, strengthening your bond.

Exercise 3: Balancing Individuality and Partnership – "Navigating New Norms"

Prompt: Write down one personal change or habit you've recently introduced into your life. Share it with your partner and discuss:

1. How does this change benefit you as an individual?

2. Does this change impact our relationship? If so, how?

3. How can we adapt or compromise to ensure this change works for both of us?

Agree on a way to support each other's individuality while maintaining balance in the relationship.

Why This Exercise Matters:
This exercise encourages mutual respect and compromise, helping both partners feel valued and supported as they grow individually.

Exercise 4: Evaluating Unexpected Shifts – "Red Flags or Green Lights?"

Prompt: Reflect on a recent shift in your partner's behavior or focus that caught you off guard. Together, evaluate:

1. Is this change strengthening or weakening our relationship?
2. Are there underlying concerns we need to address?
3. What steps can we take to manage or embrace this change in a healthy way?

Work together to create a plan for addressing concerns or supporting positive changes.

Why This Exercise Matters: This exercise encourages thoughtful discussion about changes that might otherwise create tension. It helps couples identify whether a shift is a potential challenge or an opportunity for growth.

Scripture Reflection

Scripture: *"Let each of you look not only to his own interests, but also to the interests of others."* (Philippians 2:4)

Takeaways:

1. **Selflessness Strengthens Unity:** Focusing on your partner's needs as well as your own creates harmony and understanding in the relationship.

2. **Awareness Promotes Connection:** By noticing and discussing changes, you show care and respect for your partner's journey.

3. **Collaboration Builds Trust:** Supporting each other's growth while working together ensures mutual respect and partnership.

Goal for Chapter 14:

Goal: Identify one change in your relationship—whether it's a new habit, behavior, or focus—that has caused tension. Work together to discuss its source, evaluate its impact, and create a plan to adapt or embrace it.

Chapter 15

As the World Turns

Time waits for no one, and the world continues to turn. This chapter is a reflection on the inevitable reality of aging and the changes that come with it. In a relationship, the passing of time brings both challenges and opportunities. The sooner we accept this reality and prepare for it, the better equipped we are to strengthen our bond as a couple and grow together.

Embracing the Aging Process

One of the most humbling truths about life is that as the world turns, we age. Each anniversary, each year, and each new season of life bring changes to our physical, mental, and emotional states. For some, these changes are subtle; for others, they may be more pronounced and difficult to accept.

Recently, as the writing of this book, I experienced a stroke. By God's grace, I made a 95% recovery, but it was a wake-up call—a reminder that our bodies have limits and that we must care for them. My wife has also started noticing changes in her body as she nears the age of 50, including the onset of menopause. These changes are natural and part of life, but they require acknowledgment, understanding, and adaptation.

As a couple, it's important to face the realities of aging head-on. Denial doesn't stop the clock, and avoiding discussions about health, emotional shifts, or fears related to aging can create unnecessary distance. Instead, encourage open and honest conversations about these changes. By addressing these realities together, you can foster a stronger bond and prepare for the road ahead.

Supporting Each Other Through Change

One of the greatest blessings in a relationship is having a partner who stands by you in times of struggle. When I had my stroke, my wife showed unwavering support. She cared for me without resentment or frustration, embodying the vows we made to each other.

Unfortunately, not everyone responds this way. My mother once shared a heartbreaking story about a woman who left her husband when he became seriously ill, saying, "I didn't sign up for this." These situations are sobering reminders of how vital it is to prepare mentally, emotionally, and spiritually for the unexpected.

Supporting each other through life's changes—whether they are physical, emotional, or circumstantial—is an opportunity to grow closer. It's in these moments that empathy, compassion, and unconditional love shine the brightest.

Prioritizing Intimacy and Connection

As we age, maintaining intimacy becomes even more important. Aging may bring physical limitations or health challenges, but emotional closeness and connection should remain a priority.

Intimacy isn't just about physical touch; it's about emotional and spiritual closeness. Make an effort to prioritize date nights, meaningful conversations, and moments of joy. Find new ways to connect as a couple, whether that's trying a new hobby together, taking a walk, or simply sitting down for an uninterrupted conversation.

When I was recovering from my stroke, my wife and I used that time to draw closer. It was an opportunity to deepen our connection and reflect on our shared goals for the future. It also served as a reminder to cherish the time we have together and to be intentional about creating memories.

Finding Joy in the Present

Even as the world changes around us, it's essential to find joy in the present. Celebrate the small moments—the laughter, the quiet mornings, the shared meals. Don't take the time you have for granted.

Expressing gratitude daily is one of the most powerful ways to stay grounded and connected as a couple. Be thankful for your partner, for the life you've built together, and for the opportunity to share this journey. When you focus on gratitude, it becomes easier to navigate the challenges that come with aging and the passage of time.

Long-Term Goals and Daily Gratitude

As we've discussed earlier in this book, setting goals is crucial for any relationship. Long-term goals become even more important as we age. Whether it's planning for retirement, creating a bucket list of experiences, or setting health and wellness goals, having a shared vision for the future can keep you motivated and united.

At the same time, don't overlook the importance of daily gratitude. Take a moment each day to acknowledge the blessings in your life. Thank God for your partner, for the love you share, and for the time you've been given. Life is a gift, and every moment is an opportunity to honor that gift.

Don't Take Time for Granted

The metaphor of the world turning serves as a powerful reminder that time doesn't stop. We have limited time to enjoy the life God has given us, and it's up to us to make the most of it.

So, as the world turns, commit to embracing the aging process with grace. Support each other through the changes that come with time, prioritize your connection, and find joy in the present.

Together, you can create a relationship that not only withstands the passage of time but thrives because of it.

Time waits for no one, but love and commitment can stand the test of time.

Exercises for Chapter 15: *As the World Turns*

Exercise 1: Reflect on Time – "How Are We Growing Together?"

Prompt: Individually, write down three ways you feel you've grown as a couple over the years. Then write three areas where you believe you could grow further together. Share your lists and discuss:

- How your relationship has evolved positively.
- What areas you'd like to strengthen as you continue to age.
- Set one shared goal for growth in the coming year.

Why This Exercise Matters: Reflecting on growth as a couple helps you recognize your progress while identifying opportunities to deepen your bond and address areas of improvement.

Exercise 2: Plan for Health – "Supporting Each Other's Wellness"

Prompt: Together, create a "Wellness Plan" for your relationship. Include:

1. Health goals (e.g., exercising together, scheduling regular doctor visits).
2. Emotional support strategies (e.g., weekly check-ins about stress, setting aside time to pray or meditate together).
3. Long-term planning (e.g., discussing future care needs or retirement goals).

Why This Exercise Matters: Addressing health and wellness proactively ensures that you're prepared to support each other through life's changes and challenges.

Exercise 3: Celebrating the Present – "Gratitude Practice"

Prompt: Start a "Daily Gratitude Journal" as a couple. Each day, write down:

- One thing you're thankful for about your partner.
- A shared moment from the day that brought you joy.
- A prayer or intention for your relationship. Review the journal together weekly and reflect on how gratitude has enriched your connection.

Why This Exercise Matters: Gratitude strengthens emotional intimacy and keeps the focus on the blessings in your relationship, even during challenging times.

Exercise 4: Embracing Change – "Creating New Memories"

Prompt: Make a list of 10 activities you've never done together but would like to try. They could be simple (e.g., a new recipe) or adventurous (e.g., traveling to a new destination). Choose one activity each month to explore together, and commit to making it happen.

Why This Exercise Matters: Trying new things keeps the relationship fresh and exciting while fostering deeper emotional and experiential connections.

Scripture Reflection

Scripture: "Teach us to number our days, that we may gain a heart of wisdom." (Psalm 90:12)

Takeaways:

1. **Time is Precious:** Recognize the limited time you have and make the most of every moment with your partner.
2. **Live Intentionally:** Use your time wisely by focusing on growth, love, and connection.
3. **Gain Wisdom Together:** Aging isn't just about growing older; it's about growing wiser as a couple.

Goal for Chapter 15

Goal: Choose one area (physical, emotional, or spiritual) to focus on improving together. Commit to a small, consistent action that will support growth in this area over the next month.

Chapter 16

The End of the World

As the journey of life continues, we are reminded of one undeniable truth: everything in this world has a beginning and an end. Just as we entered the world, we must eventually leave it. This is a sobering reality, but it is also an opportunity to reflect on the meaning of life, love, and the legacy we leave behind.

When we think about the end of the world—our personal world—we are faced with the fragility of life and the importance of cherishing the time we have. As couples, this realization can deepen our connection, reminding us to create lasting memories and live each moment with intention. For those of us blessed with love, the question becomes: How can we make the most of the time we've been given together?

The Reality of Mortality

It's not easy to talk about mortality, but it's a conversation every couple should have. Planning for the inevitable is not about being morbid; it's about showing love and care for one another. By preparing for the future—creating wills, health directives, and legacy plans—we ensure that our partner is cared for, even when we're no longer there.

In my own life, my wife and I have made it a priority to focus on legacy. We've worked to instill values and morals in our children, while also building something they can inherit. This isn't just about leaving behind financial security; it's about leaving behind a life that reflects the love and lessons we've shared as a family.

Living with Purpose

Knowing that life is fleeting can be a powerful motivator to live with purpose. Each anniversary, each milestone, and each small moment we share becomes a treasure. One of the greatest lessons I've learned is the importance of gratitude. Being thankful for your partner and the time you have together transforms even the simplest moments into blessings.

When I was hospitalized for the first time in my life after suffering a stroke, I saw this firsthand. My wife's unwavering support through my recovery was a testament to the strength of our bond. She didn't grow frustrated or resentful; instead, she showed me love, patience, and care. It was a reminder that love isn't just about the good times—it's about showing up for each other, even when life takes unexpected turns.

A Legacy of Love

Love leaves a legacy that transcends time. My parents, for example, shared 41 beautiful years together before my father passed away. My mother wrote a book about their journey, *The Love We Had Stays on My Mind*, which chronicled their love story and their faith-filled resilience as they faced my father's 10-year battle with cancer. That book has been a source of inspiration for me, illustrating the power of love, faith, and perseverance.

Their story reminds me that love doesn't end when a life does. It lives on in the memories, the lessons, and the impact we leave behind. For couples, the goal should be to create a love story so profound that it continues to inspire others, even after we're gone.

Finding Comfort in Faith

While the idea of the end of the world may feel overwhelming, faith offers a source of comfort and hope. The Bible reminds us that life doesn't truly end—it transforms. Through Jesus Christ, we are promised eternal life and the chance to be reunited with our loved ones in the presence of God.

Consider these scriptures that provide reassurance:

1. **John 3:16**: "For God so loved the world that He gave His one and only Son, that whoever believes in Him shall not perish but have eternal life."

159

This verse reminds us of God's promise of salvation and the eternal life that awaits those who believe.

2. **Romans 10:9**: "If you declare with your mouth, 'Jesus is Lord,' and believe in your heart that God raised Him from the dead, you will be saved."

   This is an invitation to embrace the gift of salvation and the hope it brings.

3. **Revelation 21:4**: "He will wipe every tear from their eyes. There will be no more death or mourning or crying or pain, for the old order of things has passed away."

   This promise assures us of a future without sorrow, where we will be reunited with our loved ones in a perfect, eternal world.

These verses serve as a reminder that while our time on Earth is finite, our souls are eternal. The love we share here is just a glimpse of the perfect love we'll experience in eternity.

Making the Most of the Time We Have

The end of the world doesn't have to be a source of fear; it can be a source of inspiration. It challenges us to live intentionally, to love deeply, and to prioritize what truly matters. As couples, this means making the most of each day, finding joy in the present, and building a legacy of love that will endure long after we're gone.

Here are some ways to embrace this perspective:

- **Celebrate the Present:** Don't wait for special occasions to show your love. Celebrate the everyday moments that make your relationship unique.
- **Create Lasting Memories:** Take trips, write letters, and capture moments together that will bring comfort and joy in the future.
- **Invest in Legacy:** Focus on what you want to leave behind—not just material possessions, but values, lessons, and love.

Moving Forward with Hope

As we close this chapter, let us remember that the end of the world is not the end of love. It's a transition into something greater—a reminder to live fully, love deeply, and trust in God's promise of eternity. Whether you're facing the loss of a loved one, navigating the complexities of life, or simply cherishing the time you have together, let love and faith guide your journey.

Because at the end of the world, what truly matters isn't the years we've lived, but the love we've shared.

Exercises for Chapter 16: The End of the World

Exercise 1: Reflect on Legacy – "What Will We Leave Behind?"

Prompt: Together, discuss what legacy you want to leave behind as a couple. Address the following questions:

- What values or lessons do we want our children (or others) to remember us by?
- What actions or contributions can we make now to leave a positive impact on those we love?
- How can we document our journey (e.g., writing letters, journaling, or creating family albums)?

Why This Exercise Matters: Reflecting on legacy encourages intentionality in your relationship and helps create meaningful memories that will live on beyond your time together.

Exercise 2: Plan for the Future – "Our Final Act of Love"

Prompt: Work together to create or review practical plans for the future, such as:

1. Drafting a will or estate plan.
2. Establishing health directives.
3. Discussing burial or end-of-life preferences.

Why This Exercise Matters: Planning for the future ensures that your wishes are honored and removes potential stress for your partner during difficult times. It's an act of love and consideration that strengthens trust and unity.

Exercise 3: Gratitude List – "Cherishing the Present"

Prompt: Individually write down five things you're grateful for about your partner and five things you're thankful for in your relationship. Share your lists and discuss how you can continue to nurture those aspects.

Why This Exercise Matters: Gratitude fosters appreciation for the present, deepens emotional connection, and reminds you to cherish the moments you have together.

Exercise 4: Celebrate Milestones – "Honoring the Journey"

Prompt: Plan a way to celebrate the milestones of your relationship, whether big or small. This could include:

- Recreating your first date.
- Writing letters to each other reflecting on your journey.
- Planting a tree or creating something tangible to symbolize your love.

Why This Exercise Matters: Celebrating milestones reinforces the strength of your bond and creates new memories that both partners can cherish, regardless of what the future holds.

Scripture Reflection

Scripture: "He will wipe every tear from their eyes. There will be no more death or mourning or crying or pain, for the old order of things has passed away." (Revelation 21:4)

Takeaways:

1. **Eternal Comfort:** God's promise assures us of a life without pain or sorrow, bringing hope to those who grieve.

2. **Reunion in Eternity:** Love doesn't end with death; it transcends time and space, offering the assurance of reconnection in the afterlife.

3. **Living with Purpose:** The time we have now is precious; it's an opportunity to create a legacy that reflects God's love.

Goal for Chapter 16

Goal: Identify one way to honor your relationship's legacy and commit to creating or completing it together this month. Whether it's documenting your love story, planning for the future, or simply expressing gratitude, let this action serve as a testament to the depth and strength of your love.

Final Thoughts

Finding Lasting Love in a Broken World

As the author of *How Two Love in a Broken World: A Couple's Guide to Strengthen Love and Repair the Broken Pieces*, I want to take this moment to reflect on the journey we've taken together through these pages. Much of what I've shared comes from my own personal experiences—understanding and learning about my partner, as well as coming to terms with my own brokenness.

At the start of my relationship, I didn't think I was broken. The world normalizes so many of our dysfunctions: indulgence in strip clubs, excessive drinking, toxic communication patterns—all of these are painted as "normal" by society. But as I grew closer to God, I began to see things differently. God's design for love and relationships revealed the blind spots in my life, showing me that I had internal dysfunctions I didn't even recognize.

Yet, as a couple, the goal is not to point fingers at each other's flaws. It's to grow together through every challenge. In a time when wedding vows often feel like relics of the past, and phrases like "for better or worse" or "to death do us part" are overshadowed by conditional love, it's vital to reclaim the true meaning of commitment.

Through transparency and honesty, I've shared some of my most private struggles in this book—not to entertain, but to enlighten. My nearly 27-year relationship has been far from perfect, but it's been worth every trial, every sacrifice, and every moment of growth. I want you to know that two imperfect people can come together, even in a world filled with brokenness, to create something beautiful and lasting. You can build a legacy of love for those who come after you.

The Keys to Success

To thrive in love, keep God at the center of your relationship. Both partners must embrace the journey of learning and self-improvement, asking, "How can I do better?" and "How can I grow?"

Remember, you are equal partners in your relationship—co-partners with unique roles and assignments. Whether those roles differ or overlap, the shared responsibility to love, forgive, communicate, and trust remains constant. With one direction and a unified goal, you can build a love life that reflects God's purpose for you.

A Broken World, A Renewed Mind

This world will never be free from dysfunction. The Bible reminds us that the "god of this world" is actively working to manipulate, destroy, and sow division. But that doesn't mean your relationship must follow the same path. By renewing your mind daily, as the Bible instructs us to do, you can counteract the negativity and dysfunction around you. Renewing your mind is not a one-time act—it's a continual process that strengthens your love and keeps your relationship grounded in truth.

A Final Note of Encouragement

Thank you for taking the time to read this book. I pray that it equips you with the tools, insights, and encouragement to find lasting love in this broken world. Whether you're just starting your journey or looking to strengthen a long-term relationship, know that success is possible when both partners are committed to growth and guided by faith.

Lastly, I want to share that I do offer coaching for individuals and couples. If you'd like more personalized guidance, please feel free to reach out through my website.

May you find joy, healing, and the kind of love that endures, even in the midst of this broken world.

Blessings,

Allen Brown

About the Author

 Allen Brown is the founder of Allen Brown Ministries, where his focus is on ministry outreach and publishing impactful spiritual and educational resources. His journey with Christ began in 1998 during a transformative Easter morning service, where he committed his life to the Lord and found salvation.

Married over 25 years to his devoted wife, Melissa Brown, Allen has raised four children alongside her while balancing his roles as a minister, entrepreneur, and author. His entrepreneurial journey began at the age of 12, and by 18, he had achieved significant business success, generating millions and honing his passion for leadership and financial stewardship.

Through his publishing company, Build Our Kingdom Publishing, Allen shares his insights on spiritual growth, financial wisdom, and personal transformation. His books aim to guide readers in overcoming life's challenges while applying godly principles to achieve success in every aspect of life.

Allen attributes every achievement in his life to God's faithfulness, especially during times of struggle. His ministry emphasizes the importance of trusting God, walking in faith, and applying biblical principles to experience the fullness of His promises.

In addition to his ministry and entrepreneurial efforts, Allen treasures spending time with Melissa and their four sons. Together, they reflect on his dedication to faith, family, and service, embodying his commitment to helping others grow spiritually and live lives grounded in godly wisdom and purpose.

About Build Our Kingdom Publishing

BUILD OUR KINGDOM PUBLISHING

—— BUILD OUR KINGDOM.COM ——

WE ARE A CHRISTIAN BOOK PUBLISHER WITH THE FOCUS ON PUBLISHING NON-FICTION LITERATURE TO EDIFY AND BUILD THE KINGDOM OF GOD.

OUR VISION IS TO SEE PEOPLE COME TO JESUS CHRIST AS A RESULT OF THE TITLES WE RELEASE.

FOR MORE BOOKS BY ALLEN BROWN
VISIT BUILDOURKINGDOM.COM

21 Reasons Why He Cheats on You

"Discover the Truth to Complete Your Puzzle with Your Man"

Why does he cheat? What's missing in your relationship that leaves your heart feeling incomplete? In this groundbreaking book, **"21 Reasons Why He Cheats on You,"** you'll uncover the hidden truths behind his actions and gain the insights you need to understand what's really going on.

Drawing from real-life experiences, emotional wisdom, and biblical principles, this book dives deep into the reasons men cheat, including unmet needs, emotional dissatisfaction, and more. Each chapter is designed to illuminate a key puzzle piece, helping you make sense of the pain, confusion, and heartbreak.

With clarity and compassion, this book doesn't just explain why—it guides you toward understanding, healing, and personal growth. If you've ever felt like something was missing in your relationship, this book will help you complete the picture and find your way forward.

Million Dollar Seed
How My Last $17,600
Grew to Millions God's Way

"Million Dollar Seed" tells the extraordinary journey of faith, obedience, and divine intervention that transformed the author's

final $17,600 into a thriving financial and spiritual breakthrough. This inspiring narrative goes beyond material success, exploring the profound impact of trusting God's guidance in the face of uncertainty.

The author shares candid reflections on challenges that tested and strengthened his faith. Paralleling his experiences with biblical figures like Abraham, the story highlights the timeless principles of faith and obedience in unlocking God's blessings.

Structured around three pivotal phases—life before Christ, awakening faith, and a deep trust in God—the book provides a roadmap for spiritual growth and personal transformation. More than a financial success story, "Million Dollar Seed" reveals the deeper wealth found in peace, joy, and alignment with God's purpose.

A source of motivation and practical wisdom, this book invites readers to trust in God's plan, persevere through challenges, and embrace the limitless possibilities of divine guidance.

I Will Teach You How to Hear God's Voice

In a world filled with distractions, hearing God's voice can feel elusive. Yet, the opportunity to connect with the Divine is closer than you think.

In *I Will Teach You How to Hear God's Voice,* Allen Brown draws from his own profound experiences to illuminate the path to divine communication. Through compelling personal stories and biblical wisdom, Allen unveils the life-changing power of hearing and following God's voice in every area—family, business, finances, and ministry.

This guidebook dismantles doubts and affirms that God yearns to communicate with you, guiding you toward your unique purpose. Packed with practical exercises and spiritual insights, it equips readers to cultivate sensitivity to God's whispers, interpret His silence, and deepen trust and faith.

More than a book, this is an invitation to discover a relationship with God that transforms your life. Let His voice be your guiding light.

The Christian Entrepreneur's Compass Volume 1

33 Biblical Strategies for Growing Your Business

"The Christian Entrepreneur's Compass Volume 1" by Pastor Allen Brown offers 33 powerful strategies to help entrepreneurs align their businesses with biblical principles. Drawing from timeless lessons in Scripture, Pastor Brown highlights stories of figures like Isaac, Jacob, and Joseph, transforming their experiences into actionable insights for modern business challenges.

This guide provides a unique blend of faith and practicality, encouraging readers to balance profit with purpose while building ethical, God-centered businesses. Each chapter delivers wisdom and tools to navigate today's marketplace with integrity and spiritual growth at the forefront.

Perfect for entrepreneurs, leaders, and professionals seeking to integrate their faith into their work, this book serves as a roadmap to lasting success. Whether starting a new venture or enhancing an existing one, "The Christian Entrepreneur's Compass Volume 1" inspires readers to achieve business goals while fulfilling their divine purpose.

Escape the Rat Race:
God's Way

"Escape the Rat Race: God's Way" reveals a divine path to financial freedom and spiritual abundance. This transformative guide combines biblical wisdom with practical financial insights, offering seven foundational principles—Faith, Obedience, Sacrifice, Wisdom, Resourcefulness, Gratitude, and Generosity—that lead to true prosperity as ordained by God.

More than a financial manual, this book is a roadmap to a life of purpose, fulfillment, and impact. Each chapter weaves practical advice with spiritual truths, making it accessible to anyone seeking a deeper understanding of wealth and success. It challenges conventional ideas of prosperity and invites readers to embrace spiritual richness alongside material abundance.

Whether trapped in the monotony of daily life or searching for greater meaning, "Escape the Rat Race: God's Way" inspires a shift in priorities. Experience wealth that transforms not just your bank account but your heart and spirit. Start your journey to lasting joy, peace, and divine prosperity today.

The Problem Is You
A Transformational Guide to Self-Discovery and Change

Have you ever felt stuck in your finances, career, relationships, or personal growth—wondering why success and happiness seem  just out of reach? The truth might be hard to accept: the biggest obstacle in your life is often staring back at you in the mirror.

In *The Problem Is You*, you'll uncover the hidden beliefs, habits, fears, and assumptions—the **elements of subconscious influence**—that silently sabotage your progress. Through relatable stories, practical solutions, and powerful biblical insights, this book shows how these unseen forces shape every decision and outcome in your life.

With 101 problems divided into 24 easy-to-navigate categories, *The Problem Is You* helps you identify the blind spots holding you back and empowers you to take control of your success. Whether you're facing challenges in money, relationships, career, or self-worth, this book will equip you with tools to transform your mindset and achieve lasting change.

Your breakthrough starts here.

101 Relationship Problems That Steal Your Joy

101 Relationship Problems That Steal Your Joy offers a powerful guide to overcoming the challenges that hinder joy in your

relationships. Whether you're single or in a relationship, this book addresses the problems that create emotional distance, dissatisfaction, and frustration. You'll uncover key issues, such as miscommunication, unrealistic expectations, unhealthy patterns, and the deep-rooted beliefs that prevent connection and happiness.

Each problem is explored through real-life examples, subconscious influences, and practical solutions you can start applying immediately. This book empowers you to break free from destructive cycles, build stronger connections, and foster deeper, more fulfilling relationships.

The complete guide provides valuable insights for both individuals and couples, offering actionable steps to reclaim happiness and create the love life you deserve. Don't let unresolved problems stand between you and your fulfillment. Start your journey toward a better, more joyful relationship today!

Your Life Is Not A Coincidence

Your Life Is Not a Coincidence reveals a powerful truth: the events in your life are not random—they are part of a greater  design. This transformative book introduces the **3 Pillar Perspective**, a framework that uncovers the hidden forces shaping your reality: **God's Hand**, **Conscious Decisions**, and **Subconscious Influence**.

Through personal stories, timeless wisdom, and practical insights, you'll discover how divine guidance, intentional choices, and unseen beliefs work together to create the outcomes you experience. You'll learn to recognize when God is moving in your life, make decisions that align with your purpose, and overcome subconscious patterns holding you back.

This book is your guide to understanding life's deeper meaning and taking control of your future. Nothing is by chance. When you embrace the 3 Pillar Perspective, you'll see that your life is divinely connected, purposeful, and filled with potential.

The Love We Had Stays on My Mind

The Love We Had Stays on My Mind by Dr. Carolyn Brown is a heartfelt memoir reflecting on her 41-year marriage to her late

husband, Elijah Brown. This powerful story offers a deeply personal account of their journey together, filled with love, faith, and resilience. From their serendipitous meeting to navigating the trials of life, including Elijah's battle with cancer, Carolyn provides profound insights into the strength and beauty of a lasting relationship.

Through touching anecdotes and timeless lessons, she reveals how faith and commitment carried them through life's challenges and strengthened their bond. This memoir is more than a tribute; it's a guide for readers seeking to build, sustain, or honor love in their own lives.

Perfect for those in relationships, widows, or anyone looking for inspiration, *The Love We Had Stays on My Mind* reminds us of the enduring power of love and faith.

Stop Gambling With Your Future:

Stop Gambling With Your Future: *How to Stop Gambling Addiction Through Faith and Spiritual Warfare* is a powerful guide for those seeking freedom from the grip of gambling addiction. Drawing from personal experience, author Allen Brown shares his journey of overcoming a four-year struggle with gambling through faith, prayer, and spiritual insight.

This book offers readers a comprehensive understanding of the psychological traps and spiritual battles behind gambling. It provides actionable steps, biblical principles, and practical exercises to renew the mind, rebuild trust, and reclaim control over life. Whether you're struggling with addiction yourself or supporting a loved one, this book equips you with the tools to resist temptation, break free from the cycle, and restore your purpose.

Discover how faith and spiritual warfare can lead to lasting victory, helping you rebuild your life and stop gambling with your future.

www.ingramcontent.com/pod-product-compliance
Lightning Source LLC
Chambersburg PA
CBHW071739120626
46550CB00002B/585